I0416843

MESSAGE TO JOINT WARFIGHTERS

USJFCOM has completed experiments on enabling support to widely dispersed forces, with a focus on the challenges of command and control, sustainment, and protection. This handbook describes experimentation results and includes feedback from fielded forces operating with widely distributed units. It highlights options and capabilities that can better enable units to operate in a distributed manner and discusses how commanders might consider, integrate, and support operations of widely dispersed tactical forces within a joint operations area.

Joint operations, by their nature, often employ forces widely dispersed in the operations area due to various factors such as topography, basing limitations, and unique mission requirements. In particular, the tasks assigned to ground forces can require the separation of tactical units beyond mutually supporting range of each other. The sound judgment of well trained and experienced subordinate leaders is essential to operations with widely distributed units. Part of a joint force commander's approach to supporting distributed forces may involve ways to improve tactical effectiveness of dispersed units by making select joint and component capabilities available to the lowest appropriate level.

This handbook is intended to provide a resource that stimulates the joint community's thinking on how to address the challenges associated with distributed units. We encourage you to use this handbook and to provide feedback to us on its effectiveness so that we may include these lessons learned in emerging joint doctrine, training, and professional military education.

JOSEPH REYNES, JR.
Major General, USAF
Director, Joint Concept Development &
Experimentation (J9)

STEPHEN R. LAYFIELD
Major General, U.S. Army
Director, J7 / Joint Warfighting Center

PREFACE

1. Scope

This handbook is a pre-doctrinal non-authoritative document that provides information on how JTF and component headquarters might plan for and provide capabilities to tactical units, principally battalion level and below, when they are employed widely dispersed and outside of mutually supporting range of other ground units. Although focused on ground units, there are significant implications for the air and naval components of the joint force as well. The document serves as a bridge between experimentation and current best practices and the potential incorporation of value-added ideas in joint doctrine, education, and training.

2. Content

This handbook draws on current doctrine, useful results from relevant studies and experimentation, and recognized best practices.

3. Development

This handbook is based on Service and joint lessons learned data; joint, multi-national, and Service doctrine and procedures; training and education material from CAPSTONE, KEYSTONE, and PINNACLE senior executive education programs; joint and Service exercise observations, facilitated after-action reviews and commander's summary reports; related joint concepts and experimentation results; joint exercises and trip reports; and joint publication assessment reports. The handbook also includes the results of a two-year analysis and experimentation effort requested by the United States Marine Corps (USMC) and conducted by USJFCOM, with participation by all the Services and many international partners. The experimentation campaign encompassed an analytical wargame, three constructive simulation efforts, a "human-in-the-loop experiment," and focused seminar sessions with retired senior commanders and currently serving officers with recent operational experience. The experimentation effort focused on stressing potential joint solutions in a distinctly different operational environment.

This handbook reports on various *lessons learned* and *best practices*. Chairman of the Joint Chiefs of Staff Instruction 3150.25D (10 Oct 08) codifies the Joint Lessons Learned Information System (JLLIS) as the DOD system of record for the Joint Lessons Learned Program (JLLP). JLLIS provides a Web-enabled information management system to meet the JLLP's operational needs. The JLLP provides for the transfer of knowledge within the DOD and United States Government organizations that are involved in joint operations or supported by military operations. This is done by the rapid distribution of observations and recommendations, after action reports (AAR), tactics, techniques, and procedures: topic papers, briefings, and interviews (lessons learned information). JLLIS website is at: https://www.jllis.mil or http://www.jllis.smil.mil.

4. Application

This handbook is a pre-doctrinal, non-authoritative supplement to joint doctrine that can help JTF and component commanders plan for and support operations that include the deployment and employment of widely dispersed tactical units. The information herein also helps the joint community develop doctrine and mature emerging concepts for possible transition into joint doctrine. Commanders should consider the benefits and risks of using this information in actual operations.

5. Contact Information

Comments and suggestions on this important topic are welcomed. The USJFCOM J9 points of contact are Mr. Jim Nichol, james.nichol@jfcom.mil (757) 203-3357 and Major James Righter, james.righter@jfcom.mil (757) 203-3528. The USJFCOM J7 points of contact are LTC Jim DiCrocco, james.dicrocco@jfcom.mil, (757) 203-6243 and Mr. Rick Rowlett, ricky.rowlett.ctr@jfcom.mil, (757) 203-6167.

TABLE OF CONTENTS

CHAPTER V

APPENDIX A
    CONCEPT DEVELOPMENT AND EXPERIMENTATION

GLOSSARY

FIGURES

CHAPTER I

OVERVIEW

" The future operating environment will demand the application of military power in ever-smaller increments, which in turn will require the achievement of joint synergy at ever-lower echelons of command. Joint integration that was once achieved at the component level or slightly below will be achieved routinely in the future at drastically lower echelons — even down to the small-unit level."

Capstone Concept for Joint Operations
15 January 2009

1. Background

a. This handbook is the result of study, concept development, experimentation, and analysis that began in 2005 when the Marine Corps released a white paper entitled *A Concept for Distributed Operations*. This concept was intended "…to promote discussion and to generate ideas for specific combat development initiatives" in the context of "…the irregular challenges of Small Wars." It focused on enabling small units to function with greater operational initiative and independence. In response to the concept, the Marine Corps Combat Development Command initiated a number of activities, including limited objective experiments conducted by the Marine Corps Warfighting Laboratory.

b. USJFCOM began a study of *joint distributed operations* (JDO) based on three "warfighter challenges" (*Forcible Entry* and *Distributed Operations, Lift,* and *Mobility and Sustainment*), which the Marine Corps submitted to USJFCOM J9 in 2009 and 2010 in conjunction with USJFCOM's annual *Joint Concept Development and Experimentation Campaign Plan*. As part of the USJFCOM JDO project, J9 developed an informal *Concept for Joint Distributed Operations* in November 2009. This concept and previous Marine Corps efforts informed a USJFCOM-led campaign of experimentation conducted in 2009 and 2010 intended to identify capabilities that could contribute to the successful execution of operations by widely dispersed organizations. See Appendix A for more information on concept development and experimentation.

c. This handbook identifies various issues and considerations for conducting these operations based on insights from ongoing operations and experimentation results. USJFCOM's *Joint Operating Environment*[1] (JOE) provides the future environmental context within which to examine these issues and considerations. The JOE states that "The nature of the human condition will guarantee that uncertainty, ambiguity, and surprise will dominate the course of events."[2] It continues with a conclusion that surprise will be inevitable even as joint forces prepare for a wide range of military operations, and that commanders at all levels will face complex, dynamic, and unpredictable situations for which established concepts and doctrine can

---

[1] United States Joint Forces Command, *The Joint Operating Environment*, 18 February 2010.

[2] Ibid., p. 5.

provide only a solid foundation as a point of departure. A comprehensive understanding of the current and future environment described by the JOE is essential to the development of doctrine, training, and education that will help the joint force overcome the challenges of this environment.

d. In addition to current joint doctrine, the JOE's companion document—the *Capstone Concept for Joint Operations*[3] (CCJO)—provides guidance relevant to operations by pushing select joint capabilities down to low-level units. In this handbook, see paragraph 1a in Chapter IV and paragraph 2c in Appendix A for CCJO references.

2. Context

a. Joint operations are, by nature, distributed across the operations area. The joint force's Service components are typically separated geographically due to factors such as topography, basing availability, overflight rights, and unique mission requirements. Special operations forces (SOF) have historically operated in a distributed manner in support of joint operation planning and execution. However, cross-domain support within the joint force, such as the air, SOF, and naval components' support for ground components, is "standard procedure" and is achievable in most circumstances. Likewise, other commands typically support the joint force from distant locations as well.

b. From the ground component commander's perspective, however, it is typically undesirable to distribute ground units beyond the range at which they can mutually support each other in any operation where combat is likely. Nonetheless, operational circumstances and tasks assigned to ground components can require the wide separation of their tactical units within large operations areas. This has often occurred historically, as in Vietnam, and is the case in ongoing operations today.

> *"Our current study of the conflicts in Afghanistan and Iraq offers us lessons as well. In order to combat a decentralized enemy, we've learned—relearned—that we have to decentralize capabilities and distribute operations."*
>
> GEN Martin E. Dempsey
> "Mission Command"
> Army Magazine, January 2011

c. The challenges identified during experimentation with respect to widely dispersed ground component units can complicate joint operations, degrade the effectiveness of the joint force, and increase operational risk. When such separation occurs, the higher Service or functional component commander and joint force commander (JFC) must compensate to prevent widely separated units, and the joint force as a whole, from operating at unreasonable risk. Support of

---

[3] Department of Defense *Capstone Concept for Joint Operations* (CCJO) Version 3.0, 15 January 2009, contains a "joint operating precept" that centers on pushing joint capabilities down to the lowest level at which they can be effectively used.

these units beyond their organic capabilities can be essential to the joint force's success. **Thus the focus of this handbook is on the support required to facilitate operations by units widely distributed in the operations area.**

d. **The term** *distributed operations* **does not refer to a specific type of joint operations.** However, such operations are characterized by a joint force's Service or functional component subordinate elements operating widely dispersed and often beyond mutually supporting range. *Mutually supporting range* typically refers to units that are geographically close enough to support each other with at least indirect fire and can move or maneuver soon enough to reinforce each other with direct fire and maneuver. Such support can be essential to a unit that has an opportunity to exploit circumstances that will accomplish its mission as well as to a unit that is decisively engaged[4] and at risk of defeat. Combat operations in these circumstances can have support implications that span all joint functions and require quick response. If the joint force and component headquarters can support these operations effectively in combat, they should be able to do likewise in less intense operations involving security, relief and reconstruction, and peacetime engagement.

A Squad operating away from a Forward Operating Base (USMC photo)

---

[4] FM 1-02/MCRP 5-12A, *Operational Terms and Graphics*, September, 2004, p. 1-53. In land and naval warfare, ***decisive engagement*** is an engagement in which a unit is considered fully committed and cannot maneuver or extricate itself. In the absence of outside assistance, the action must be fought to a conclusion and either won or lost with the forces at hand.

e. The JFLCC's decision on how to employ forces in the operations area is driven primarily by the terrain, the adversary, tasks assigned by the JFC, and available resources. Current counterinsurgency operations in Afghanistan are reflective of small units operating within large operations areas. In these operations, unlike strikes and raids, battalion commanders often are tasked to establish presence and maintain influence and control over geographic areas that are far larger than in the past. It is not uncommon for company areas of operation to be spread throughout a large battalion operations area in a nonlinear arrangement that does not provide for common boundaries with other companies. These units often operate independently[5] and well beyond mutually supporting range of other ground units.

f. Operations of widely dispersed units, with additional capabilities deliberately pushed to subordinate headquarters or made available as required, have become more common. An assessment of recent operations reveals that commanders are doing their best to provide widely dispersed tactical formations with adequate intelligence, sustainment, reliable command and control connectivity, responsive fires, and the direction and intent that empower small units while still providing clear left and right limits. Our successes are attributable to commanders and staffs who have exercised good judgment, have tailored their organizations to act more independently and, perhaps most importantly, have made available and employed a wide variety of non-organic capabilities to make these widely dispersed units more capable. Recent successes are also due, in part, to the wealth of resources available to the joint force today. This was not always the case and may not be in the future.

g. This handbook is not intended to address the tactics of ground units, but it identifies issues and offers considerations for how the joint force and Service (or functional) component headquarters can exploit opportunity, balance risk, and empower widely dispersed tactical formations.

(1) For context, **Chapter II** provides a simple vignette of operations by a three-star joint task force (JTF) headquarters reporting to a combatant command headquarters. The vignette focuses on considerations for supporting the land component commander's widely distributed battalion headquarters and companies. The issues and considerations discussed in Chapters III and IV relate to supporting these dispersed units engaged in operations likely to involve combat. The chapter presents operational design and joint operation planning considerations and addresses factors that influence a decision to operate with widely separated forces. The three most significant factors are: (1) the mission and longer-term desired outcomes; (2) the operational environment; and (3) the resources that will be made available to the joint force.

---

[5] "Independent," used infrequently in the handbook, is meant to describe a set of circumstances that requires units to operate well outside the range at which they can readily support each other and potentially in an environment where communication with the next higher commander is problematic. Nonetheless, leaders in these circumstances make decisions and operate consistent with the philosophy of *commander's intent* and *mission command* as joint doctrine describes. Commander's intent helps widely dispersed units operate with a common purpose. It should enable mission command at all levels and allows subordinates the greatest possible freedom of action. It should provide focus to the staff and help subordinate and supporting commanders act to achieve the commander's desired results without further orders once the operation begins.

(2) **Chapter III** identifies a number of issues that are particularly important to supporting these operations. It uses an organizing framework of the six joint functions (*command and control*, *intelligence*, *fires*, *movement and maneuver*, *protection* and *sustainment*). As conditions and activities change, so will those factors and conditions that affect our ability to provide responsive joint support to widely separated tactical units. These considerations reflect much of what the joint force has learned over time, particularly while executing recent and ongoing contingency operations.

(3) **Chapter IV** identifies operational implications and discusses changes that could be made to joint doctrine, training, professional military education, and other areas to formalize and enable joint force and component support to dispersed tactical units. **Chapter V** provides concluding thoughts.

Counterinsurgency Patrol Leader speaking with local Afghan in Helmand Province, Afghanistan (USMC photo)

(4) **Appendix A** provides additional background on concept development and experimentation that have examined various aspects of distributed operations, particularly with respect to the types of external supporting capabilities that can enable these operations and reduce risk to dispersed forces.

h. The handbook mentions various capabilities that can support operations by widely dispersed units. *Capabilities* relate to organizations and systems that can support or be provided to distributed units. The joint force's Service components should provide some of these capabilities, while the joint force headquarters can provide or coordinate for others. **The chart on the next page provides examples of capabilities mentioned in this handbook.**

Distributed Operations Sample Supporting Capabilities

- Establish a Joint Aerial Layer Network (JALN) to improve communications by providing persistent bandwidth to distributed unit.

- Colocate fires capabilities with dispersed units (e.g., joint fires observer, joint terminal attack controller, tactical air control party, air liaison team).

- Push surveillance and fires-capable unmanned aerial vehicles (UAV) such as Predator and Reaper (and their ground stations) down to distributed units.

- Increase presence of liaison personnel (who should come with organic transportation and communications) with distributed units.

- Locate foreign disclosure officers to provide greater access to distributed units to facilitate information sharing with interorganizational partners.

- Form a specific staff organization, such as a joint interagency coordination group (JIACG), and focus its efforts on facilitating coordination with interorganizational partners down at the level of distributed units.

- Establish regional information centers and locate them to facilitate information gathering and sharing among distributed units.

- Provide distributed units with joint contracting assistance in contracting for host nation and third party support.

- Coordinate for USTRANSCOM's air and sea JTF port opening (JTF-PO) capabilities to establish air and/or sea ports to support distributed operations.

- Enhance the Service component's resupply capabilities by coordinating for use of Joint Precision Air Drop System (JPADS), los-cost/low-altitude (LC/LA) resupply, and Defense Logistics Agency tailored logistical support (e.g., Class VIII medical push packages and vehicle preventive maintenance kits).

- Establish joint security areas (JSA) and joint security coordination centers (JSCC) to enhance regional protection.

- Coordinate for the Joint Public Affairs Support Element (JPASE) and the combatant commander's communication strategy experts to help enhance the JTF and component commanders' communication strategies to ensure consistent use of themes and messages by distributed units.

CHAPTER II

OPERATIONAL DESIGN AND PLANNING

> *"First, in designing joint operations, the joint force commander must come to grips with each operational situation on its own terms, accepting that this understanding rarely will be complete or entirely correct, but at best will approximate reality."*
>
> *"In this environment, the joint force cannot afford to apply preconceived methods reflexively, but instead must conform its methods to the specific conditions of each situation."[6]*
>
> **Capstone Concept for Joint Operations**

1. Introduction

a. Joint operation planning is a problem-solving process, no matter what the nature of the mission, the echelon of command, or the operational circumstances. It ties the military instrument of national power to the achievement of diplomatic ends, and is essential to securing diplomatic outcomes during peace and war.

b. Operational design is a creative process that complements planning and helps commanders and planners understand and relate ends, ways, means, and risk before executing military operations. Operational design and planning begin with the end in mind, providing a unifying purpose around which actions and resources are focused. In particular, operational design focuses early on the broad visualization of potential solutions to the problem at hand so as to provide the best possible guidance for detailed planning. This chapter highlights considerations that are particularly relevant early in operational design and planning when circumstances require operations by widely dispersed units.

2. Context

a. The hypothetical JTF mentioned in Chapter I is organized as Figure II-1 depicts. The three-star commander of JTF (CJTF) BLUE reports to the combatant commander (CCDR). Army and Marine Corps units operate under a JFLCC. Special operations forces under a subordinate JSOTF operate throughout the JTF commander's joint operations area (JOA) rather than within a designated joint special operations area. The JFC designates

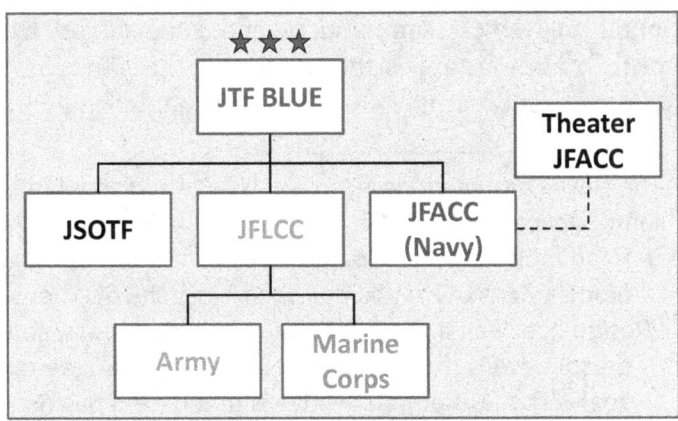

Figure II-1. JTF Organization

---

[6] *Capstone Concept for Joint Operations*, p. 12.

the Navy component[7] commander as the JFACC for JTF BLUE with additional support from the CCDR's theater JFACC as required. The Navy component commander also provides maritime support, which is minimal in this scenario. Another JTF (GREEN) is operating concurrently in a separate JOA elsewhere in the CCDR's area of responsibility (AOR).

b. The hypothetical scenario involves operations against a credible insurgent force operating throughout the large JOA that encompasses the country's borders. **Country Gray** (the host country) military forces have been ineffective against the insurgent, and the country's government is steadily losing public support. Typical of contemporary operations in Afghanistan, this force is not a peer competitor of US forces. But the insurgent has several advantages, including detailed knowledge of the country and the ability to hide in plain sight among the population. It also has sufficiently modern C2 capabilities and weapons to conduct effective (but short-duration) local combat engagements against US forces. The purpose of this scenario is only to describe a situation that could lead to the wide distribution of US ground forces. The scenario is not intended as a vehicle to debate counterinsurgency nuances.

3. Operational Design

a. *Operational design* is the conception and construction of the intellectual framework that underpins joint operation plans and their subsequent execution.[8] It blends with the complementary joint operation planning process to produce the eventual plan or order that drives the joint operation. Early in operational design the CJTF Blue and staff (in collaboration with components) focus on developing or enhancing their understanding of the *operational environment*[9] and the specific *problem* that requires the commitment of US forces. In the JTF Blue scenario, a short-notice contingency operation, operational design begins concurrently with mission analysis.[10]

b. The operation order (OPORD) that CJTF Blue receives from the CCDR is a key initial driver that helps frame the CJTF's understanding of the environment and problem. CJTF Blue might tend to expect that the higher headquarters has correctly described the operational environment, framed the problem, and devised a sound approach to achieve the best solution. But strategic guidance can be vague, and the commander must interpret and filter it for the staff. While CCDRs and national leaders may have a clear strategic perspective of the problem, operational-level commanders and subordinate leaders often have a better understanding of specific circumstances that comprise the situation. Both perspectives are essential to a sound solution. Subordinate commanders should be aggressive in sharing their perspective with their

---

[7] The Navy component is a carrier strike group supplemented by limited multinational naval capabilities.

[8] Joint Publication (JP) 1-02, *Department of Defense Dictionary of Military and Associated Terms*.

[9] Defined in JP 1-02 as, "A composite of the conditions, circumstances, and influences that affect the employment of capabilities and bear o the decisions of the commander."

[10] **Design** has been a topic of study for several years, and perspectives differ on its application. One perspective is that *design* is separate from the detailed planning process and occurs prior to mission analysis. Another perspective is that design begins as part of mission analysis. Joint doctrine aligns with the second perspective. See JP 5-0, *Joint Operation Planning* (Final Coordination draft as of 25 Oct 10), for details on operational design and its interaction with the joint operation planning process.

superiors early in design, and both should resolve differences at the earliest opportunity. The JFLCC's distributed employment of forces throughout an extensive JOA Blue will likely create additional support requirements for the CJTF and perhaps for the CCDR as well. CJTF Blue and component commanders and staff collaborate on these requirements as early as possible in order to determine if the CJTF should request additional resources.

Task Force 2/7, Afghanistan, 2008

Distributed operations can create opportunities to extend the joint force's influence and control by employing tactical units in a widely dispersed manner. For example, in 2008, the 1300 personnel of Task Force 2/7, built around the Second Battalion of the Seventh Marine Regiment, operating in Afghanistan, "...were assigned an area of operations of more than 28,000 square kilometers -- roughly the size of Vermont."[11] Whether by design or out of necessity, tactical ground units (battalion and below) are assuming responsibility for far larger operating areas than at any time in the past.

---

c. A course of action (COA) that distributes ground forces widely throughout the JFLCC's area of operations (AO) can become evident to the JFLCC early in operational design, as will other possible COAs. In this hypothetical scenario, insurgent forces have freedom of movement and are operating throughout the country, although larger operations focus on one region and outlying operations are relatively sporadic. While the JFLCC might be inclined initially to favor a dispersed approach in this case, many other factors that should be considered early in design will indicate whether a "distributed" COA is even acceptable and feasible. For example, the host nation government's agreement to the employment of US forces may contain restrictions that affect force employment options. Likewise, the level of host nation support for basing, contract labor, transportation, certain classes of supply, and other factors will affect deployment and initial employment timelines. In this scenario, the support requirements of another JTF operating elsewhere in the CCDR's AOR will compete with those of JTF BLUE, which could affect the availability of JFLCC and joint assets necessary to enable distributed ground operations.

d. If it is obvious to the JFLCC that the situation calls for wide distribution of ground forces, the JFLCC's staff can begin planning for the additional functional support required to sustain, protect, and reinforce these forces even before detailed COA wargaming and comparison begin. A potential dispersed employment option for ground forces should be evident to the JFC, since early operational design is a highly collaborative effort between the joint force and component headquarters. In addition to supporting conventional ground operations, the CJTF and staff must also consider the unique support required for SOF operations. Thus the JFC and staff can also begin early to identify joint capabilities that might be pushed lower to further enable ground units.

e. As the CJTF and staff gain an understanding of the problem within the context of the operational environment, potential broad alternatives should become evident. The CJTF and staff use their understanding of the current operational environment, the nature of the problem, and

---

[11] Oliver North, "The Heartland of the Enemy," August 15, 2008.

how the environment should look when operations conclude to develop a broad solution called the *operational approach*. This is a visualization of general actions, typically described in text and graphics using *lines of effort* and *lines of operations*, to produce conditions that will achieve the desired *end state*.[12] The operational approach should describe operational objectives that will enable the joint force to create the key conditions of the desired end state.

f. CJTF Blue will provide the operational approach, together with *commander's intent*, as part of the *commander's planning guidance* that drives follow-on detailed planning. Figure II-2 shows CJTF Blue's broad operational approach for this operation. It is based on four primary and 12 subordinate lines of effort that should create the conditions necessary to achieve the desired operational environment when operations conclude.

g. Even if CJTF Blue and the JFLCC conclude that strategic objectives and the CJTF's assigned tasks require dispersed ground operations, the operational approach will not describe the details. Commanders and staffs will develop, analyze, and compare alternative COAs during subsequent detailed planning. **CJTF Blue's primary task, which is reflected in the desired end state, is to work with Country Gray's government and military to defeat the insurgency and set the conditions for support of the population and long-term stability**.

h. Following approval of the joint force's mission statement CJTF Blue issues planning guidance. This guidance includes the problem definition, description of the operational environment, the initial intent statement, and the CJTF's operational approach, which the joint force and component staffs will use as the basis for COA development. An extract of the operational approach is below, and is followed by Figure II-2 that depicts four major lines of effort.

JTF Blue Commander's Operational Approach

The JTF COS has convened the component commander's and staff. CJTF Blue describes the following operational approach as part of his planning guidance:

The purpose of this campaign is to help the established government in Country Gray defeat the ongoing insurgency and restore stability to the country. This will help restore stability in the region, which is in our vital national interests. The desired end result is a country free of insurgency and a populace that accepts and supports the established government.

Our approach to our mission will be along four major lines of effort, each having subordinate supporting lines. Our first priority — the Security line of effort — is to protect the population and then contain and defeat the insurgency. Concurrently we will begin training host nation security forces so that they can quell any resurgence of unrest once we leave the country.

---

[12] Defined in JP 1-02 as, "The set of required conditions that defines achievement of the commander's objectives."

The main effort on the Security LOE will initially be on combat operations in Alpha Province, since insurgent activities and C2 are concentrated there. However, the insurgents are operating at various levels throughout Country Gray, so MG Smith (the JFLCC) has recommended that our approach must involve concurrently deploying into and operating in all regions throughout the JOA. The JFLCC must accept more risk in this approach, since many ground units would be widely separated, particularly in the outlying regions. This will stress land component and joint C2, intelligence, and sustainment capabilities, and will significantly extend JFACC operations. However, a distributed approach will also establish relations and influence with province and village leaders more quickly, and should provide a level of security they don't currently have. I believe the potential value of these relationships outweighs the additional risks of the approach. However, I have told the J5 to develop at least one valid non-distributed COA for comparison while we continue to expand our understanding of the operational environment and the fundamental nature of the problem. On this LOE, the JSOTF will focus initially on identifying and eliminating key insurgent leaders throughout the JOA.

Three other lines of effort are essential to this operational approach............
..CJTF Blue's description continues)

Vignette continues later in this chapter

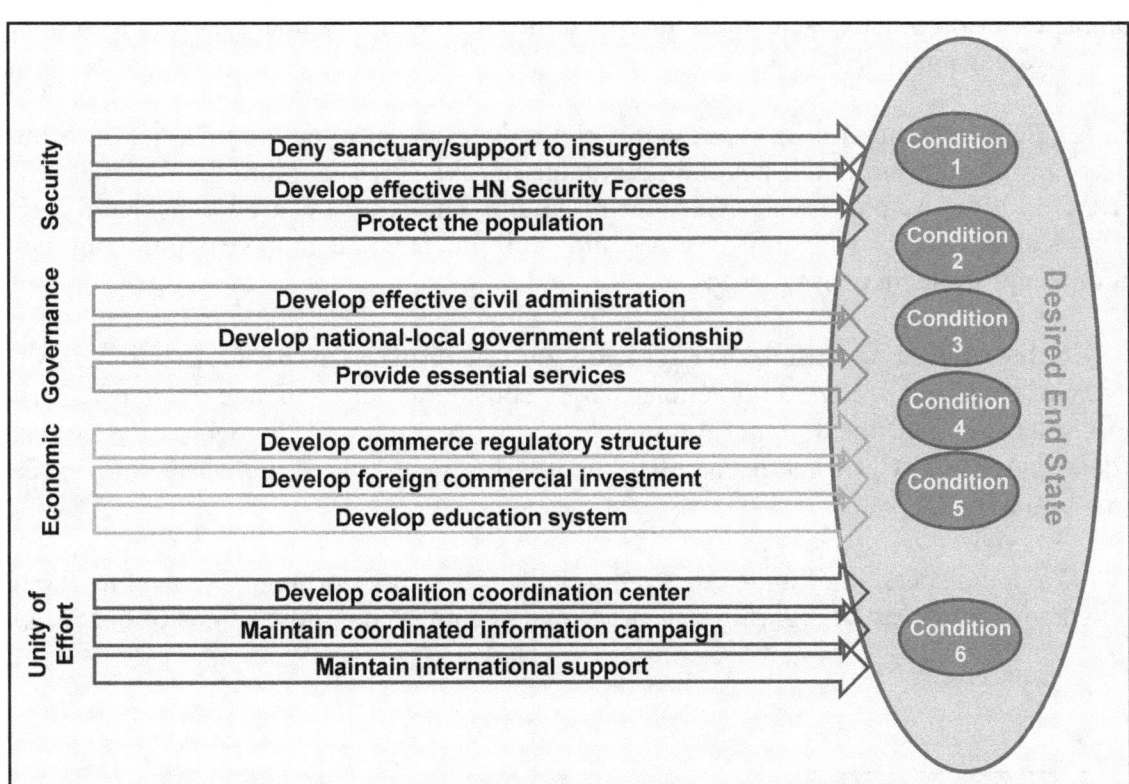

Figure III-2. Sample Operational Approach

4. Joint Operation Planning

a. The joint operation planning process (JOPP) is an orderly, analytical process that consists of a logical set of steps to analyze a mission; develop, analyze, and compare alternative courses of action against each other; select the best course of action; and produce a joint operation plan or order.[13] When operational circumstances constrain planning time, operational design and JOPP begin concurrently.[14]

b. During planning, all COAs selected for analysis must be valid (*adequate, feasible, acceptable, distinguishable*, and *complete*).[15] The planning process and many planning considerations for operations with dispersed units are the same as for those other types of operations and employment methods. Following are examples of considerations that must be addressed during planning with respect to employing widely distributed ground forces. The JFLCC might have options or capabilities to address these challenges or enhance the potential benefits, but support from the CJTF's level may be required as well. Chapter III addresses considerations by functional area.

(1) Combat increases the risk to distributed ground units, since these units are not positioned to reinforce others. **An increased risk to ground units translates to increased mission risk for the ground component and the joint force.** This consideration challenges the *acceptable* criterion of COA selection, for which the commander balances a COA's cost and risk with the advantage gained.

(2) Both active and passive measures can reduce risk. An active measure is to increase capability provided a unit, well beyond its organic capabilities. A more passive measure is to craft ROE to give the unit greater freedom of action. The latter must be considered carefully, since tactical actions, however necessary and well intended, can have significant negative operational and strategic consequences.

(3) **Distributed operations are typically more complicated**, particularly in terms of *C2, sustainment, fires,* and *protection* functions. These considerations challenge the *feasible* criterion of COA selection (and the *simplicity* principle of joint operations), for which the commander must determine if the COA can accomplish the mission within the established time, space, and resource limitations.

(4) Wide dispersion of units creates the challenge of monitoring and managing the terrain between them, which can be significantly larger than the units' individual areas of operations.

---

[13] JP 1-02. Also, see JP 5-0 for details of JOPP steps.

[14] See footnote 32. During peacetime planning, circumstances will typically allow the commander and staff to focus on the visualization aspects of design without the time-constrained requirement to complete mission analysis and press on with detailed planning.

[15] JP 5-0. See Figure III-6 and discussion on page III-28 in the 26 Dec 06 approved JP.

(5) Known *operational limitations*[16] (such as *rules of engagement* (ROE)) may affect distributed employment.

(6) The CJTF, component commanders, and staff must consider all aspects of sustainment as they develop the initial operational approach. They must wargame logistics alternatives during COA development and analysis, since restrictive terrain, lack of infrastructure, and enemy activity can greatly affect normal logistics methods and processes.

(7) Dispersed employment can increase the commander's opportunity to influence key leaders and the population throughout the JOA and ground AOs when such influence is important to mission accomplishment. This can have a beneficial effect on the commander's *communication strategy*.[17]

(8) Dispersed employment can increase situational awareness and provide more opportunities for leveraging human intelligence throughout the JOA and ground AOs.

(9) Extended separation between units complicates joint and component commanders' "on-the-ground" assessments with subordinate leaders.

(10) Widely dispersed units may negatively affect the joint force's interaction with interorganizational partners[18] with respect to communications and mutual support.

(11) The JFC must balance the advantage of dedicating joint capabilities to distributed ground units against the reduced ability to react responsively elsewhere with these capabilities.

(12) Distributed employment can negatively affect the joint force's interface with supporting commands and other organizations.

---

[16] Defined in JP 1-02 as, "An action required or prohibited by higher authority, such as a constraint or a restraint, and other restrictions that limit the commander's freedom of action, such as diplomatic agreements, rules of engagement, political and economic conditions in affected countries, and host nation issues."

[17] JP 3-0, *Joint Operations*, Revision Final Coordination Draft, 7 October 2010. This publication will establish *communication strategy* as a new term with the following definition: "A commander's strategy for coordinating and synchronizing themes, messages, images, and actions to support strategic communication objectives and ensure the integrity and consistency of themes and messages to the lowest tactical level."

[18] JP 3-08, *Interorganizational Coordination during Joint Operations*, Revision Final Coordination draft, 9 June 2010. "**Interorganizational partners**" is based on a new doctrinal term that refers collectively to US Government (USG) departments and agencies; state, territorial, local, and tribal government agencies; foreign military forces and government agencies, intergovernmental organizations (IGOs), nongovernmental organizations (NGOs); and entities of the private sector.

Extract of CJTF Blue's COA/CONOPS Briefing

Several days after CJTF Blue presented planning guidance, which included the operational approach, the COS convenes the staff and component commanders to discuss the approved COA and issues related to the concept of operations. This extract does <u>not</u> focus on the details of the LOEs listed in Figure II-2. Instead it highlights some of the challenges facing the JTF based on the commander's selection of a distributed approach to the mission, and it provides examples of how a commander might address those challenges. The CJTF leads the discussion.

You should recall from my earlier planning guidance that I approved an initial operational approach based on the early deployment and employment of ground force units throughout the land component commander's AO. We wargamed this approach as well as two other potential COAs that deployed forces in greater concentration to two provinces, and then secured other provinces consecutively. Our analysis validated all three COAs. Two are safer than the distributed approach that deploys units concurrently to all provinces, which carries more risk. While they will accomplish our mission, however, the alternative COAs will take longer and will not address some of the fundamental underlying problems that stimulated the insurgency in the first place. If we don't help the country's leadership resolve these issues, our efforts may not set the conditions for the long-term stability the region needs. Also, we might be back here in three years to solve the same problems. Therefore, I agree with MG Smith (the JFLCC) and I approve the distributed COA based on the operational approach. I've discussed this with the combatant commander, who agrees the potential benefit trumps the additional risk. In spite of JTF Green's competing requirements (a JTF elsewhere in the AOR), the CCDR will give us another infantry brigade to be OPCON within a week of our initial deployment.

Obviously MG Smith's CONOPS is key to the JTF's success. With no appreciable air or sea threat, the land component will be the main effort throughout the operation. Before we discuss the details of deployment and employment, I want to highlight some of the challenges associated with the distributed approach and how we intend to overcome them.

A top priority is to reduce the risk associated with the noncontiguous nature of ground operations in this operational environment. The terrain isn't as rugged as Afghanistan, but the provinces are large, road networks poorly developed, and the rainy season will not be our friend. MG Smith's CONOPS will deploy most of the battalions in his four brigades and one MEU throughout the ground AO. This puts a lot of boots on the ground, but it also leaves a lot of territory uncovered in which the insurgents can hide. We've received more intelligence on the enemy in the last few days, and we now know that the insurgent is stronger in numbers and more widely deployed than we anticipated. Security for dispersed units will be a 360-degree challenge, and responsive support for them across the functions is a high priority.

Most battalions will be outside mutually supporting range of each other unless helicopter lift is immediately available, and the JFLCC's artillery cannot range the entire AO even if the batteries are dispersed. CAS will be the only joint fire support for some of our units in the outlying provinces. We will push as many joint fires observers, TACPs, and air liaison elements as possible to the ground component, and MG Smith is developing a priority list of units that get these capabilities based on the current intelligence picture. The J2 and J3 are also coordinating for surveillance- and fires-capable UAS and their ground stations. The surveillance UAS can help us increase the coverage where we have no immediate physical presence. I want these assets pushed down also, but we must have an effective plan to secure and sustain them.

Sustainment will challenge both Service and joint capabilities. MG Smith is assessing how much additional helicopter support he needs. We will establish forward operating bases and forward arming and refueling points for both logistics and fire support purposes. Each base must be positioned so that assets using them can cover as many dispersed company HQ and platoon bases as possible. The J4 and division G4 are working with the Defense Logistics Agency for tailored logistical support push packages. Most resupply outside of 50 miles from Capitol City will likely be by helicopter or airdrop. JPADS (Joint Precision Air Drop System) *availability is limited because JTF GREEN has priority, but the J4 is coordinating for remaining systems and MG Smith will determine their best use. With these, we can resupply directly to company-level bases. The J4 and land component G4 are researching opportunities for host nation support to help dispersed units with food, water, and other requirements, but outlying provinces are pretty austere. The JTF HQ will work with MG Smith to provide joint contracting support as low as possible to help contract for HNS and third-party support. Responsive medical support is a high priority, and the push packages will include Class VIII. MG Smith is looking at using something similar to the Marine's "shock trauma platoon," which will deploy with the MEU, to support widely distributed Army units in treating casualties that don't require immediate evacuation from the AO.*

Converting information from a large number of sources into actionable intelligence is a challenge. We need to get a clear picture of the insurgent's key locations and capabilities as quickly as possible. Since the JFLCC will be the main effort throughout the operation, I'm going to locate the NIST (National Intelligence Support Team) *at MG Smith's HQ rather than at the JTF HQ. I have also asked the CCDR for some additional intelligence support, and he is sending three intelligence officers and supporting analysts to us for the duration of the operation. My intent is to create two regional intelligence cells forward in the operations area. These will work with designated brigade and battalion HQs, analyze and share information between the two cells, and send results to both the JFLCC and the JTF HQ intelligence shops. I expect this approach to facilitate intelligence processing, exploitation, and dissemination.*

The combatant commander's AOR communication strategy already contains themes and messages that relate to this operation. My communication strategy amplifies these and reinforces specific points that I believe are essential to addressing the country's underlying problems. Our forces must be consistent in conveying these messages to the lowest level, and seeking the right opportunities to counter the insurgent leaders' messages. I'm sending the JTF HQ's communication strategy folks to visit with all battalion commanders before we deploy to ensure our leadership is on the same page. The increased support of Country Gray's people for their government and our operations is at the core of the conditions we must set to achieve success. USJFCOM's JPASE (Joint Public Affairs Support Element) *will join us in the JOA, and will help us maintain the right visibility of this effort by sending PA experts to visit battalion HQs once battalion bases are established. They also can advise battalion and company commanders on how to handle specific challenges related to PA.*

We know that we will be collaborating with the State Department and other interorganizational partners early and throughout operations, particularly in the provinces close Capitol City. I don't expect much interaction initially in the outlying provinces, but activity will increase later when we defeat the insurgency. As this interaction occurs, I have coordinated with MG Smith to send JTF HQ interagency experts directly to battalion HQs to help commanders coordinate with interorganizational partners.

Finally, we all know that operations may not go as expected, communications may fail at the worst moment, and our junior leaders will have to make immediate decisions on their own. I believe my commander's intent is clear and we have a solid operational approach and CONOPS for this operation. Make sure your subordinate commanders and leaders understand this intent at low levels so that they can make good decisions consistent with this intent if communications fail. I know that we have good junior leaders and we have reinforced the tenets of mission command in our training and other operations. I'm confident that this should serve us well in our current mission.

If there are no questions, let's move on to discuss operations along each line of effort.. .

(Commander's CONOPS discussion continues)

5. Assessment

a. *Assessment* is a continuous process that measures the overall effectiveness of employing joint force capabilities and the progress toward accomplishing a task, creating an effect, or achieving an objective during military operations.[19] It begins during early operational design as commanders and staffs consider measures by which to determine progress. Commanders continuously assess the operational environment and progress of operations, and compare the results to their initial vision and intent.

b. In a general sense, the assessment process applies to operations with distributed ground forces just as to any other operation. However, the commander may give special assessment emphasis to some aspects of operations based on the potential risk inherent to operating with small widely distributed units in the operational area. Following are examples.

(1) If the JFLCC chooses a COA that widely distributes forces when there are other valid COAs, the staff should devise assessment measures to compare the progress during distributed

---

[19] JP 1-02. Also, refer to JP 3-0 and JP 5-0 for more information on assessment, measures of performance, and measures of effectiveness.

execution to the progress expected if an alternative COA had been executed. COA analysis, wargaming, and comparison can help identify appropriate measures. For example, a potential purpose of distributing units is to increase the force's influence on key civilian leaders and population in the area. The staff should develop measures to indicate progress toward the leaders' and population's acceptance of the CJTF's communication strategy themes and messages.

(2) Given the noncontiguous nature of unit boundaries during distributed operations, the staff should devise measures to determine if surveillance ways and means are sufficient for monitoring terrain gaps between units.

c. **The staff also should develop *redesign criteria* during assessment.** These are specific criteria that not only measure progress toward objectives, but they also indicate the possibility of significant changes in the operational environment, the problem, or both that could cause CJTF Blue to reconsider whether the current operational approach is viable. Redesign criteria should support the commander's ability to understand, learn, and adapt, and could lead to a redesign effort that produces a revised or new operational approach (particularly if progress is unsatisfactory). Since distributed ground operations are typically more complicated and risky, the commander should keep alternatives close at hand and plan for options to mitigate risk.

This Page Intentionally Blank

CHAPTER III

FUNCTIONAL AREA CONSIDERATIONS

"We're finding that almost all higher HQ are pushing assets and capabilities down to the tactical level while increasing the overall capacity for information sharing, reach back, and federation to maintain common situational awareness across the force. Confusion can occur if these "pushed down" assets and capabilities continue to also receive taskings from their parent organization while under the guise of supporting the designated tactical unit. Recognizing the value of these assets to multiple customers, we observe that a unity of effort approach normally improves synergy and harmony, particularly when combined with transparency and clear priorities of support."[20]

General (retired) Gary Luck
"Joint Distributed Operations: Insights"
10 February 2010

1. Introduction

a. When tactical units are widely dispersed, network connectivity becomes more difficult and vulnerable. This can affect each of the six joint functions (*command and control, intelligence, movement and maneuver, fires, protection,* and *sustainment.*)[21]

(1) A more decentralized approach to command and control may be in order. Feedback from experimentation and ongoing operations suggests that commanders may have to task-organize differently, and, in some cases, augment small units, including SOF, with non-organic capabilities and the means to employ them.

(2) The management of intelligence, surveillance, and reconnaissance (ISR) assets and the collection and dissemination of information and intelligence to empower widely separated ground units becomes even more important.

(3) The ability to maneuver, concentrate, disperse, and provide protection is problematic as conditions change.

(4) The ability to provide responsive ground-based fires becomes difficult across extended operations areas, particularly when maneuver units cannot support each other.

---

[20] General (Ret.) Gary Luck and Colonel (Ret.) Mike Findlay, "Joint Distributed Operations: Insights", 10 February 2010.

[21] JP 3-0. See discussion of joint functions beginning on page III-1.

(5) Many aspects of protection are more complicated by the extended gaps between units. The flank security required in contiguous operations becomes a 360 degree problem between noncontiguous units.

(6) Sustainment becomes more demanding as units operate over extended lines of communication (LOCs). Medical evacuation (MEDEVAC) planning and execution may have to be done differently to account for extended distances and the number of widely dispersed units in the operations area. Moreover, operating widely dispersed puts a greater premium on our ability to effectively leverage and support a broad range of potential partners.

b. In short, supporting the employment of widely dispersed forces creates additional demands across the joint functions that the JFC and component commanders must address in design, planning, and execution. Not the least of these demands is the challenge of effectively balancing priorities for functional support to widely dispersed units. There will typically be high demands on limited joint resources, and the joint force might not even represent the main effort in the CCDR's AOR. This chapter identifies a variety of issues and considerations related to operations with widely dispersed units. Some considerations apply primarily to the joint and senior component HQ, while other considerations apply at the low tactical level. All are important to a well-integrated approach to conducting and supporting distributed operations. They are organized using the six joint functions — *command and control*, *intelligence*, *movement and maneuver*, *fires*, *sustainment*, and *protection* — although many issues overlap more than one function.

"Companies, even platoons, under junior leaders became the basic units of the jungle. Out of sight of one another, often out of touch, their wireless blanketed by hills, they marched and fought on their own, often for days at a time. They frequently approached the battle in scattered columns, as they did for the crossings of the Irrawaddy, and concentrated on the battlefield. The methods by which they did this and, above all the qualities they needed to make these tactics possible and successful repay study. They may be needed again."

Field-Marshal Viscount Slim
Commander, British XIVth Army
Defeat Into Victory

---

2. Command and Control[22]

a. Command and control is the "…exercise of authority and direction by a properly designated commander over assigned and attached forces in the accomplishment of the mission."[23] Commanders and their staffs perform this function through an arrangement of

---

[22] Text box quote is from Field-Marshal Viscount Slim "Defeat Into Victory," 1956. P. 542.
[23] JP 1-02.

personnel, equipment, communications, facilities, and procedures during planning, directing, coordinating, and controlling forces and operations.

The Winter War
Finland in Distributed Operations, 1939-1940

The Winter War was a military conflict between the Soviet Union and Finland. It began with a Soviet offensive on 30 November 1939—three months after the start of World War II and the Soviet invasion of Poland—and ended on 13 March 1940 with the Moscow Peace Treaty. The League of Nations deemed the attack illegal and expelled the Soviet Union on 14 December 1939.[24]

The Soviet forces had three times as many soldiers as the Finns, 30 times as many aircraft, and a hundred times as many tanks. The Red Army, however, had been crippled by Soviet leader Joseph Stalin's Great Purge of 1937, reducing the army's morale and efficiency shortly before the outbreak of the fighting. With more than 30,000 of its army officers executed or imprisoned, including most of those of the highest ranks, the Red Army in 1939 had many inexperienced senior officers. Because of these factors, and high commitment and morale in the Finnish forces, Finland resisted the Soviet invasion for far longer than the Soviets expected.[25]

In this 1939-1940 winter war, the Finns successfully employed widely distributed forces against less mobile Soviet columns, inflicting disproportionate casualties upon a numerically superior foe. The Finns used an operational design that relied on independent actions and a mobility advantage to generate a string of

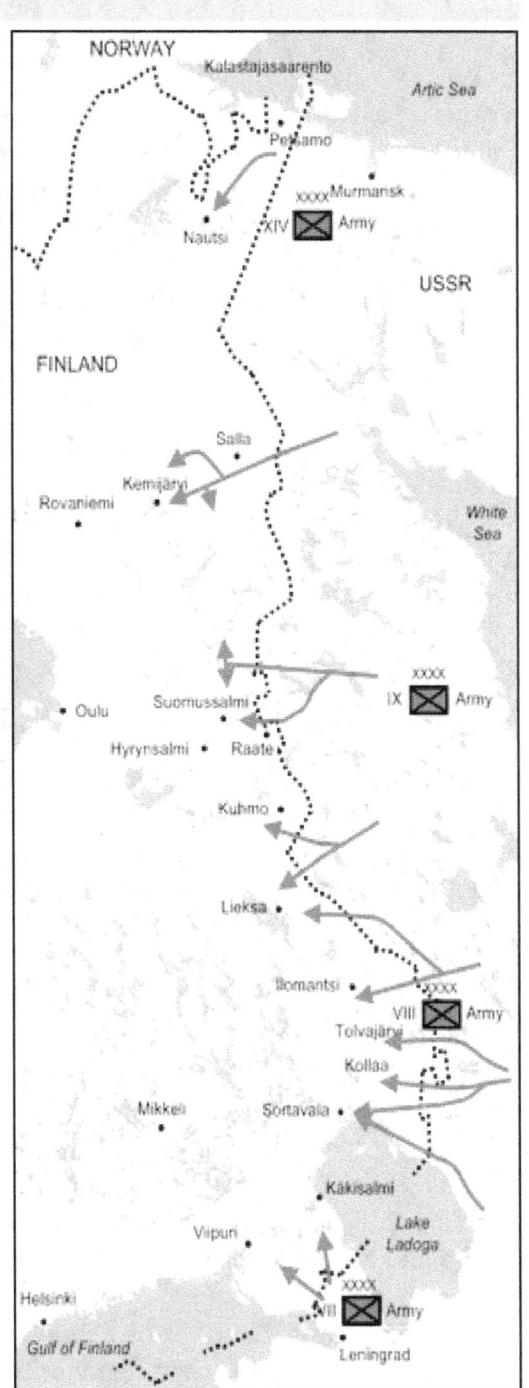

---

[24] http://en.wikipedia.org/wiki/Winter_War. This vignette is summarized from the Wikipedia article *Winter War*, which contains citations for primary sources.
[25] Ibid.

tactical-level successes. In some engagements, the small units of the Finnish Army fought semi-autonomously, but were guided by a common understanding of the operational aim. The superb individual proficiency of the Finnish soldiers and their junior leaders served as a force multiplier that raised the combat power of their forces well beyond that represented by mere numbers of personnel and quantities of equipment.[26]

b. Widely dispersed action in distributed operations reinforces the importance of mission type orders, clear commander's intent, and concise C2 arrangements together with well-understood priorities of effort. **To be most effective, these operations will also require decentralized decision-making and empowerment of subordinate leaders.** The objective is to increase agility and initiative at the tactical level. Widely distributed units might require capabilities beyond their organic C2. How these capabilities are made available depends, in large part, on the C2 relationships established by higher authority. The following paragraphs discuss C2 considerations grouped in the following categories: *unified action*; *mission command*; *communications considerations*, and *information management considerations*.

c. **Unified Action.** Important when determining C2 arrangements at all levels is how to synchronize, coordinate, and/or integrate the activities of governmental and nongovernmental entities with military operations to achieve unity of effort.[27] This requires joint forces to work closely with a significant number of external stakeholders collectively referred to as *interorganizational partners*. These include, but are not limited to, US interagency partners, host nation civilian and military organizations, non-governmental organizations, and international organizations. These "external" partners might help support widely distributed operations by assisting the affected units. For example, widely distributed company-sized units could benefit greatly by host nation support for food and fresh water resupply, which would ease the component HQ's sustainment requirements. Conversely though, distributed units may be required to enable the work of these interorganizational partners, as would be the case if a private volunteer organization requested assistance with security issues. Following are some key insights and considerations for developing a more effective approach to unified action in these operations:

(1) The JFC should consider forming a specific staff organization, such as a joint interagency coordination group (JIACG), and focus its efforts on facilitating coordination with interorganizational partners down at the level of dispersed units.

(2) Unit leaders must work with the other members of the national security team in the most skilled, tactful, and persistent ways to promote unified action. The agencies' different and sometimes conflicting policies, procedures, decision-making processes, organizational cultures, and nature and extent of resourcing complicate this interface.

(3) Integration and coordination among distributed units and interorganizational counterparts is much less rigid than military C2. Likewise, some organizations may have policies that oppose those of the US military. Formal agreements, robust liaison, and

---

[26] USMC *A Concept for Distributed Operations*, p. IV.
[27] Ibid.

information sharing with interorganizational partners are options that should facilitate common understanding, coordination, and mission accomplishment.

(4) Military terminology can inhibit effective communication between military units and interorganizational counterparts. Rather than *command and control*, these partners will be more comfortable with terms such as *coordination, consensus, cooperation, collaboration, compromise, consultation,* and *deconfliction.* JP 3-08, *Interorganizational Coordination during Joint Operations,* discusses this range of terms that describe the interaction that may occur among partners. Unit leaders at the lowest level should understand this framework.

(5) Building interpersonal relationships with external partners is as important as building them within US military organizations. Distributed operations will often require small unit leaders to establish and foster these interpersonal connections. Company commanders and platoon leaders must know how to reach out to potential partners at the first opportunity, and must maintain beneficial relationships throughout the operation.

(6) Understanding partner and stakeholder roles, authorities, goals, processes, procedures, and culture facilitates interorganizational collaboration. Developing this understanding is an added requirement for small unit leaders whose time and attention are already thinly stretched, but it is essential to effective collaboration.

(7) Interorganizational stakeholders may expect that units will provide military and other forms of support. Commanders must anticipate these requirements, which might have to be addressed and managed at small unit level, but could create additional resource issues counterproductive to the mission. Liaison with interorganizational counterparts is essential to enable US military leaders to fully understand the partners' capabilities and limitations. Commanders must ensure they do not obligate US agencies and other partners to provide sustained support without proper coordination and agreement.

(8) Interagency and international partners have relatively limited capacity to support multiple distributed units. Small unit leaders must appreciate the strengths and limitations of their partners. Higher authority must help manage expectations of both distributed units and their partners in the operations area.

(9) Dispersed units may need to reorganize (and possibly expand) their command posts to facilitate communications with and between an extensive array of interorganizational partners.

(10) Combined Joint Task Force Horn of Africa (CJTF-HOA) is one example of a JTF that is facilitating unified action. CJTF-HOA's combined JOA includes six countries and one failed state. It is also conducting operations in six other counties outside the JOA. To facilitate unified action, CJTF HOA deploys a small *Country Coordination Element* to most US embassies in the region to coordinate joint planning and execution. The elements help ensure the respective Chiefs of Mission and the JFC synchronize all USG activity in the region.

(11) In Iraq, US Forces Iraq (USF-I) works in close coordination with the US Embassy in Baghdad, and has developed an overarching and effective framework to gain unity of effort.

o The joint development and implementation of the *Joint Campaign Plan* is co-signed by the USF-I Commander and US Ambassador to Iraq. This plan serves to better integrate and coordinate activities between widely dispersed units, each operating with an extensive array of external partners.

> *"(A)cting without orders, in anticipation of orders, or without waiting for approval, must become second nature in any form of warfare where formations do not fight closely en cadre, and must go down to the smallest units. It requires in the higher command a corresponding flexibility of mind, confidence in its subordinates, and the power to make its intentions clear right through the force."*
>
> **Field-Marshal Viscount Slim**
> **Commander, British XIVth Army**
> **<u>Defeat Into Victory</u>**

o The co-location of the USF-I J9 staff in the embassy itself. The J9 is functionally organized across campaign plan lines of operations to match the country team organization. This structure has enabled the J9 staff to establish strong relationships within the embassy staff and better support the country team's lead role in the *political*, *economic and energy*, and *rule of law* lines of operations.

d. **Mission Command**. *Mission command* is the conduct of military operations through decentralized execution based upon mission-type orders.[28] Successful mission command demands that subordinate leaders at all echelons must be able to exercise disciplined initiative and act aggressively and independently to accomplish the mission. Under mission command, commanders issue mission-type orders and use implicit communications. They delegate decisions to subordinates wherever possible, which minimizes detailed control and empowers subordinates' initiative. The typical operational circumstances of distributed operations make mission command essential to success.[29]

(1) Fundamental to mission command is the thorough knowledge and understanding of the commander's intent at every level of command. *Commander's intent* is a clear and concise expression of the operation's purpose and desired end state.[30] Commander's intent should enable mission command and allow subordinates the greatest possible freedom of action. It should provide focus to the staff and help subordinate and supporting commanders act to achieve the commander's desired results without further orders once the operation begins, even when the operation does not unfold as planned. Successful mission command demands that subordinate leaders at all echelons exercise disciplined initiative, and act aggressively and independently to

---

[28] JP 1-02.
[29] Quote in text box below is from Slim, p. 542.
[30] JP 1-02.

accomplish the mission within the commander's intent. Commanders focus their orders on the purpose of the operation rather than on the details of how to perform assigned tasks. Subordinates' emphasis is on timely decision-making, understanding the higher commander's intent, and clearly identifying the subordinates' tasks necessary to achieve the desired end state. It improves subordinates' ability to act effectively in fluid, chaotic situations. Although not crafted as an intent statement, many of the items in Figure III-1 provide a clear perspective on COMISAF's recent intent for counterinsurgency operations (COIN) operations in Afghanistan.

Commander, ISAF COIN Guidance

- Secure and serve the population
- Live Among the people
- Help confront the culture of impunity
- Help the Afghans build accountable governance
- Pursue the enemy relentlessly.
- Fight hard and fight with discipline
- Identify corrupt officials
- Hold what we secure
- Foster lasting solutions
- Money is ammo; don't put it in the wrong hands
- Consult and build relationships, but not just with those who seek us out

- Walk
- Act as one team
- Partner with the ANSF
- Promote local reintegration
- Be first with the truth
- Fight the information war aggressively
- Manage expectations.
- Live our values
- Maintain continuity through unit transitions
- Empower subordinates
- Win the battle of wits
- Exercise initiative
- Be a good guest

ISAF – International Security Assistance Force

Figure III-1. Commander, ISAF COIN Guidance

(2) Mutual trust, understanding, and confidence shared between senior and subordinate leaders are indispensable to distributed operations and fundamental to empowering subordinates. The trust and mutual understanding developed in training allows subordinates to know what is expected of them and how their actions integrate into the wider purpose of the commander's vision. Once confident that subordinates know how to innovate appropriate action based on commonly discussed principles, commanders must exercise the restraint that enables the innovative potential of subordinates to take effective action in chaotic and complex situations. Building trust and confidence is a deliberate action. It must be planned for, actively built through words and actions, and continually reinforced. Successful commanders build personal relationships and inspire trust and confidence, while leveraging the analytical ability of their staffs.

(3) Commander's build subordinates' trust and confidence in part by interacting with them. As CJTF Blue and the JFLCC travel throughout the operations area, they gain a more refined appreciation for the tactical situation their subordinate commander's are facing.

o Tactical leaders are each wrestling with a different portion of the operational problem in different ways. They exchange information laterally to enhance their situational understanding, and inform their commander of tactical circumstances and exploitable anomalies in their area of operations. CJTF Blue and the JTF staff digest these many insights and points of information to discern operational patterns and glean opportunities to seize the initiative and exploit advantage.

o Coincident with battlefield circulation and other means of disseminating intent, the commander discusses with subordinates a continuously developing appreciation of the situation in Country Gray. The commander discusses relative strengths and weaknesses, reflects on the dynamics of the operational problem and deepens his junior leaders' insight into both the operational situation and the CJTF's thoughts on how can gain and maintain the initiative. These conversations allow the commander to articulate expectations and project the force of personality to subordinates.

o The iterative nature of design and planning is predicated on commander's intent informing the action and initiative of subordinates, and subordinate 'feedback' on the results of their efforts informing the senior commander's subsequent intent and guidance. Senior commanders share thoughts with subordinates on how to achieve advantage, and they solicit junior leaders' thoughts on developing creative solutions to tactical and operational-level problems. CJTF Blue and the JFLCC incorporate their appreciation of enemy intentions, capabilities, and vulnerabilities and their subordinates' proposed solutions, and then continue to refine the operational approach, even during execution. This reciprocal and collaborative process contributes significantly to the development of mutual understanding and enables subordinates to act with initiative, assured that their actions are in accord with the commander's overarching intent.

> *"When all is said and done, it is really the commander's coup d'oeil, his ability to see things simply, to identify the whole business of war completely with himself, that is the essence of good generalship."*
>
> **Carl von Clausewitz**
> **On War**

(4) Empowering widely dispersed subordinates to act on trust and confidence of their leaders and the philosophy and authority of mission command may often require additional capability. Later parts of this chapter provide examples of specific capabilities associated with other functions, but the decisions on if, when, and what capabilities to provide rest with the C2 function (see Figure III-2). *Speed of trust* can be influenced by *speed of decision*, particularly considering the increased time-distance factors that affect support for widely distributed units. Each function can benefit by development of a suite of effective decision support tools tailored

for specific protection, sustainment, intelligence, and other requirements associated with distributed operations.

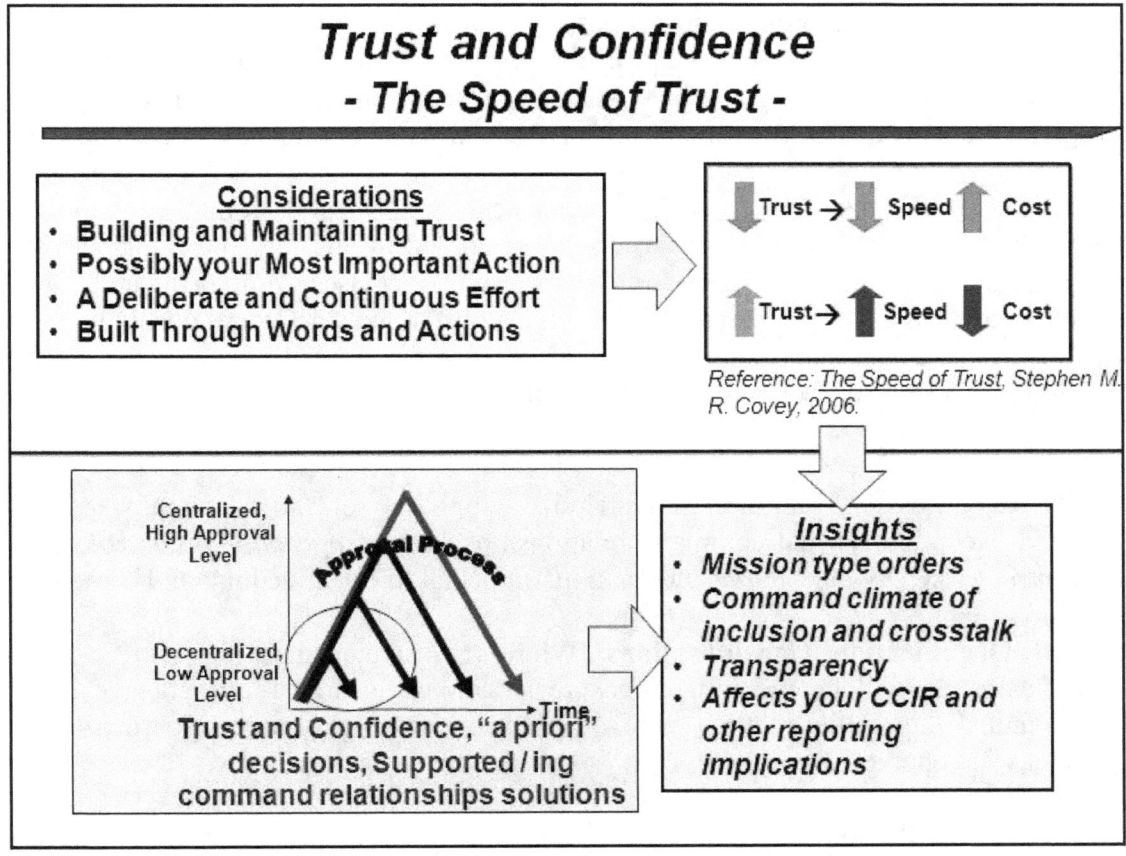

Figure III-2. Trust and Confidence – The Speed of Trust

o   The units envisioned in widely dispersed ground operations are not authorized an extensive array of organic capabilities. For example, an Army infantry battalion does not have organic artillery, and typically relies on the brigade's artillery battalion for indirect fire support (other than the infantry battalion's mortars). Some widely dispersed units may be well beyond the range of artillery support, and immediately responsive close air support (CAS) could be problematic as well. When circumstances dictate, component and joint force commanders should provide control of relevant supporting capabilities to the lowest appropriate level capable of integrating and employing the assets effectively. An example would be locating an artillery battery from the brigade's artillery battalion in an isolated infantry company's operations area in direct support of the company's operations. *Control* of these capabilities must include the ability (e.g. people, processes, systems, and authorities) to employ them. Higher HQ prioritization and risk assessment are essential, since many distributed units could benefit by these scarce resources.

o   Small unit commanders may not always know when or whether to ask for additional capabilities beyond standard "support" requests (such as MEDEVAC and CAS). The philosophy of mission command does not preclude higher commanders from closely monitoring tactical operations. Component and joint commanders should anticipate when tactical circumstances might require "pushing" such capabilities to distributed units, and be proactive when the need is apparent.

o Lateral coordination increases the joint force's agility in some respects, because it creates potential opportunities for distributed units to share non-organic capabilities. This coordination is essential even when a unit is outside mutually supporting range of other units' organic maneuver and fires capabilities. For example, one infantry company in control of a fires or intelligence-capable unmanned aerial vehicle could release control to another company on short notice if the need arises. This is consistent with mission command philosophy to empower subordinates and let them make decisions guided by the higher commander's intent. Lateral coordination stimulates information sharing and increases component and joint force situational awareness. "We're finding that almost all higher HQ are pushing assets and capabilities down to the tactical level while increasing the overall capacity for information sharing, reach back, and federation to maintain common situational awareness across the force".[31]

(5) Regardless of mission command's emphasis on trust, empowerment, and decentralized execution, formal command relationships such as *operational control* (OPCON), *tactical control* (TACON), and *support* remain instrumental to effective joint and component C2.

e. **Staff Organization Considerations**. While the fundamental HQ staff organization applies, adjustments will be required to ensure situational awareness, responsive support to distributed units, and unified action with a variety of interorganizational partners dispersed throughout a wide operations area.

(1) The distribution of small units throughout a large operations area will increase demands on higher HQ. Decentralized execution notwithstanding, the joint force and senior component HQ staffs require continuous visibility of unit actions so as to ensure situational awareness and responsive support. They must be more proactive and prepared to push capabilities lower in some situations rather than waiting for requests. The staff should have a system in place to dynamically re-task capabilities to ensure near real-time responsiveness to the distributed units. Clear, flexible supporting and supported relationships are essential. The JFC's staff must understand the JFC's and higher commander's intent and act accordingly in the commander's absence.

(2) USF-I's J9, mentioned earlier, is an example of a staff adjustment to orient a portion of the staff on external partner and stakeholder coordination. Depending on the extent of interorganizational partners' presence in the operations area, a staff section like this should consider not only how these partners can be leveraged by distributed units but also what demands may be placed on these units by these external partners.

(3) Widely distributed units can increase the requirement for LNOs. Exchange of LNOs provides for close, continuous, physical communications between organizations. They monitor, coordinate, advise, and assist in operation planning conducted by the organizations to which they

---

[31] General (Ret.) Gary Luck and Colonel (Ret.) Mike Findlay, "Joint Distributed Operations: Insights", 10 February 2010.

are assigned. Carefully selected, well qualified LNOs promote unity of effort, enhance interoperability and contribute significantly to mission success.

f. **Communications Considerations.** Assured communications are always important, but the requirement to distribute small units widely throughout a large operations area can place additional demands on communications planning and systems.

(1) Lateral (peer-to-peer) communications processes facilitate sharing relevant information and resources rather than exclusively using the vertical chain of command to obtain information. Requiring all echelons to establish internet relay chat procedures could help units keep up with dynamic situations when other methods of communication are unavailable or inadequate. Effective lateral communications depend on clear commander's intent.

(2) A joint force that employs widely dispersed units needs a robust, multi-tiered (surface, space, and aerial layer) network that provides adequate coverage. Such a three-tiered network will improve communications by providing persistent bandwidth to distributed units, as well as the capability and capacity to meet the critical communication and collaboration requirements of interorganizational partners. This additional "air layer," the Joint Aerial Layer Network (JALN), can make extensive use of coalition air platforms as well as our own. Deliberate planning and dynamic management, which will have to be centralized at joint force level with highly inclusive oversight processes, will be required to coordinate these assets.

(3) The aerial layer will create a degree of friction if not carefully managed. Many of the platforms tasked to support the JALN as communications nodes will be multi-mission platforms. Even as these aircraft support the network, they will be responding to other tasks as well. Close coordination with the JFACC is necessary to ensure that non-dedicated capabilities are leveraged when the opportunity presents. However, these assets must be requested with due regard to the potential degradation of other missions for which these same aircraft are responsible. As currently configured, JALN can only operate in a permissive air threat environment. Solutions are needed for operations when threats to air operations are present.

(4) The JALN concept also supports enhanced information transport and increased availability by providing greater network redundancy. However, the increased robustness of the network will not eliminate vulnerabilities, reinforcing the need for mission type orders for potentially isolated units.

(5) An innovative approach currently being used in operational theaters gives joint forces access to systems that allow real-time information exchanges between different tactical data-link systems. An airborne system provides a communications relay and gateway (which functions both as a "translator" between different systems as well as providing reach back via SATCOM) and is flown at extremely high altitudes. A fixed-wing aircraft employing the system allows special operations forces to communicate with other distributed forces that are beyond line of sight. This is a significant force multiplier that enhances mission effectiveness when units are operating in mountainous, urban, or other areas where line-of-sight communication is degraded. This capability has non-combat applications as well. It can be used to allow aid convoys or

dispersed relief and reconstruction teams to stay in continuous contact via the gateway reach-back while in adverse terrain.

g. **Information Management (IM) Considerations.** *Information management* is the process of managing an organization's information resources for the handling of data and information acquired by one or many different systems, individuals, and organizations in a way that optimizes access by all who have a share in that data or a right to that information.[32] IM continues to be one of the greatest challenges for our joint forces. Distributed operations may magnify this challenge, but they also offer great advantages. Gathering and disseminating useful information can reduce the degree of uncertainty, and *pattern recognition* can help bound the range of variability in enemy response and even anticipate or estimate a probability of enemy action. However, nothing can "solve" the inherently uncertain nature of war. How we choose to deal with the abundance of uncertainty is a principle driver of distributed operations. As noted military author Martin Van Creveld indicates in his works, it is a relatively binary choice. We can centralize uncertainty and attempt to deal with it holistically, or we disaggregate the wider problem into smaller, and more discrete and resolvable parts. While these smaller component "tactical" problems will share the emergent nature of the operational problems, their complexity will be proportionately reduced by a diminished number of stakeholders in a smaller geographic area. By distributing rather than centralizing uncertainty, patterns of enemy action and stakeholder interest should become apparent sooner, sequentially reducing the opaqueness of one piece of the overall operational puzzle at a time. By decentralizing the decision-making process and increasing the number of decision makers grappling with the operational problem, we simultaneously distribute uncertainty into more manageable and resolvable parts. Perhaps more simply stated, dispersing more of our trained and experienced small unit leaders throughout the AO puts more "eyes on the situation," which should improve the intelligence picture, more rapidly reduce uncertainty, and enhance the joint force's responsiveness to the developing situation.

(1) While the traditional vertical decision and authority lines are the bedrock of military operations, current information sharing and collaboration processes are network-enabled and inclusive in nature. Information flow is instantaneous and ubiquitous and allows for rapid collaboration and sharing among numerous HQ, agencies, and staffs. Figure III-3 compares traditional decision lines and information-sharing collaboration lines.

(2) The joint force may now be more vulnerable given its dependence on networks. This condition of "digital dependence" is a potential single point of failure in contested cyberspace. Consideration should be given to maintaining proficiency in less vulnerable forms of communication such as high frequency (HF) radio. Commanders must consider other alternative ways and means if primary capabilities fail. They must also consider the significance of commander's intent under degraded or denied communications environments.

(3) Unified action with our interorganizational partners requires effective information sharing. However, various restrictions apply to sharing information with these partners. Small unit leaders will be involved in managing what they can share with multinational military

---

[32] JP 3-0 Revision Final Draft. This definition is a revision of the current approved definition in JP 1-02, and will replace that definition when JP 3-0 is approved.

partners (which could include classified information), while they also must adhere to tighter restrictions on what they can share with other interorganizational partners. While greater transparency with partners is encouraged, leaders must ensure that restrictions are clear and conveyed to the lowest levels. The employment of US foreign disclosure officers at lower levels can facilitate this process.

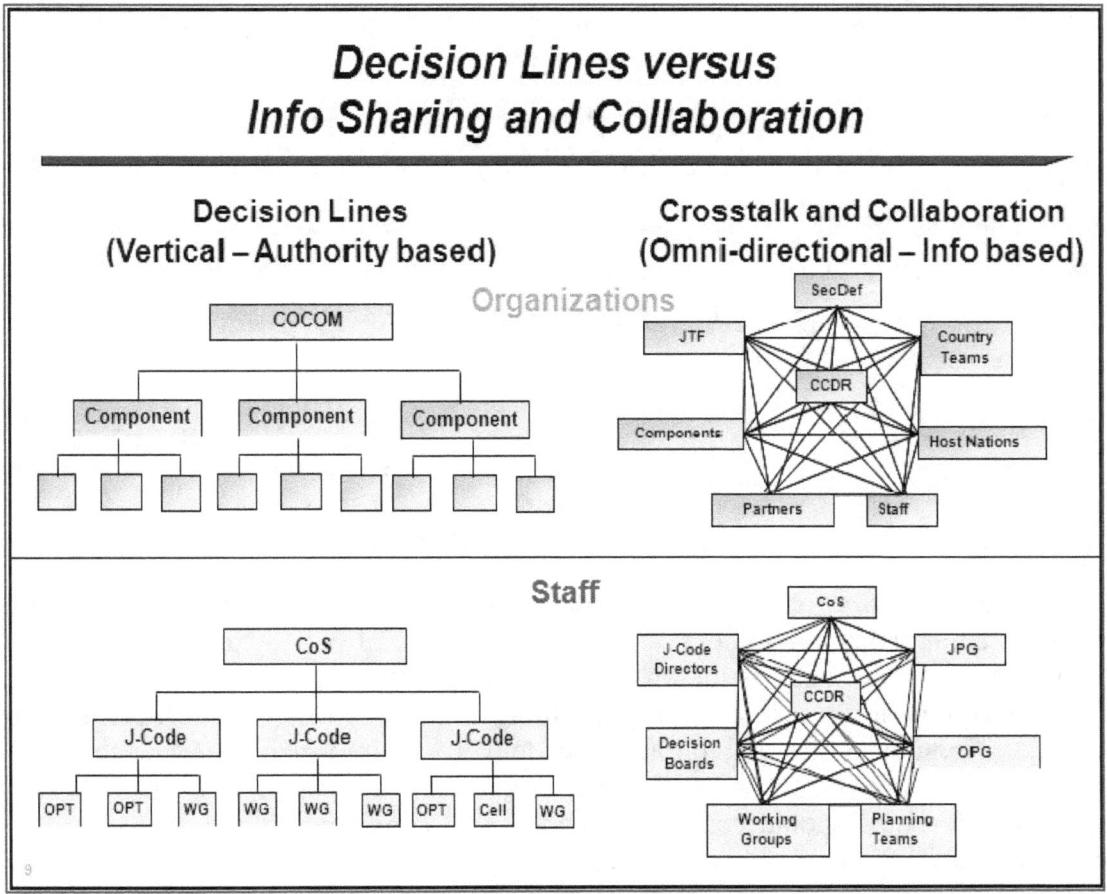

Figure III-3. Decision Lines Versus Info Sharing and Collaboration

(4) A large number of small units located throughout the operations area will act provide more "points of information" for higher headquarters. While this can enhance the joint force's overall situational awareness, the volume of information that could be generated may require that analytical capabilities be provided at lower echelons. This additional capability will become a resource issue for the JFC or Service component. Likewise, more information flowing up can generate more requests for information from higher HQ, which could detract from the units' primary tasks.

(5) Through *strategic communication* (SC), the US Government focuses efforts to understand and engage key audiences to create, strengthen, or preserve conditions favorable for the advancement of our national interests, policies, and objectives. Strategic communication programs use various themes, messages, and products to influence these audiences. At combatant commands and below, commanders use their *communication strategy* to implement

strategic communication requirements.[33] Information actions in a distributed environment rely heavily on junior leaders who thoroughly understand and properly execute their commander's communication strategy. This means that what a platoon leader or company commander discusses with a local tribal or province leader with respect to the unit's mission and the US intentions must be consistent with the themes and messages in the higher commander's communication strategy. It also means that the unit's actions, which typically are more influential than the commander's words, must also be consistent with approved themes and messages.

Communication Strategy – A Definition

"A commander's strategy for coordinating and synchronizing themes, messages, images, and actions to support strategic communication objectives and ensure the integrity and consistency of themes and messages to the lowest tactical level."

JP 3-0, *Joint Operations*
(Revised Final Coordination Draft,
7 October 2010

---

(6) Observations from recent military operations clearly show the need for a commander's communication strategy that is both an integral part of the commander's larger overall strategy and that supports the broader interagency strategic communication effort. The commander's communication strategy must promulgate the commander's message, synthesizing all means of communication and information delivery to inform and influence the various audiences and be complementary and reinforcing of the interagency effort. The JFC and component commanders should consider establishing a commander's communication strategy working group to integrate communications strategy with the staff assessment, planning, execution and assessment process.

Higher HQ' information operations message "...did not apply to all AOs and could have [had] a negative impact." For example, HQ wanted one unit to deliver a message about a government seed program, but the program was not available in the local area."

Company Commander
2nd Battalion, 8th Marines Unit Debrief

---

[33] Strategic communication and communication strategy are defined in JP 1-02 and described in JP 3-0. For details, see US Joint Forces Command Joint Warfighting Center *Commander's Handbook for Strategic Communication and Communication Strategy* Version 3.0, 24 June 2010.

(7) Distributed units will often serve as the delivery means for the commander's message, reinforcing the importance of understanding the higher commander's intent and communication strategy. Small unit leaders, operating well away from supporting units and with limited oversight, will represent the mission and the message to a whole host of different actors. One example of this challenge from a USMC company commander in Afghanistan is listed in the text box above.

3. Intelligence

a. *Intelligence* is the product resulting from the collection, processing, integration, evaluation, analysis, and interpretation of available information concerning foreign nations, hostile or potentially hostile forces or elements, or areas of actual or potential operations.[34] Intelligence operations evolve over time and vary based on requirements to best support operational and tactical level decision-making and execution. Today's operations, often against non-state actors and transnational threats, range from combat (often at small unit level) to security, stability, and humanitarian support.[35] Intelligence organizations in the field are changing to support the dispersed nature of such operations. Figure III-4 shows one example of how the focus of the intelligence effort shifts over time.

Figure III-4. Intelligence Organization

---

[34] JP 1-02.

[35] General (Ret.) Gary Luck and Colonel (Ret.) Mike Findlay, Joint Operation and Best Practices Insights, July 2008.

b. Distributed operations offer unique advantages when the decision maker is closer to the source of intelligence. Decentralized decision-making at the tactical edge is inherently faster and more dexterous than that of remote centralized decision authorities, especially in geographically dispersed and complex environments. By virtue of maintaining constant observation and longer orientation in proximity to the enemy or problem, the on-scene tactical decision maker is capable of more intuitive and rapid decisions than a remote senior, and is closer to the directed action to observe any variance from the intended result. Consequently, both speed and fidelity of action and adaptation to circumstance are enhanced by proximity of decision. The awareness to adapt subsequent actions to immediate and hard-earned lessons further enables greater tactical dexterity. Decentralized decisions can be faster when speed is imperative to retain the initiative. However, with more time the same decision maker can provide a significantly more localized, tailored, textured, and nuanced action, meeting the increasing demand for adaptation and dexterity required in complex operations. This inherent advantage also brings new challenges.

c. This section will provide key insights about intelligence requirements necessary to support operations when units are widely dispersed.

(1) JFCs and lower echelon commanders should expand their view of the environment beyond the military threat with the knowledge that a truly comprehensive understanding of the operational environment will be difficult to attain. Gaining understanding and situational awareness will require collaboration with various interorganizational partners. Although units below battalion do not have organic intelligence officers, companies and platoons are often key intelligence-gathering nodes in the intelligence system because of their low-level interface with interorganizational partners. Recognizing this, both the Marine Corps and the Army are placing more emphasis on company-level intelligence capabilities. The JFC and component commanders should consider how to support these low-level efforts.

(2) The JFC must consider adding host nation information requirements to the traditional focus areas of priority information requirements and friendly forces information requirements. Host nation information is that which the commander needs about friendly nation institutions or organizations in order to partner effectively, develop plans, make decisions, and to integrate military operations with civilian activities.

(3) By virtue of the force's extended posture, dispersed units offer greater opportunity to collect information and intelligence, since each individual can serve as an intelligence collector. However, this extended posture and resulting expanded collection opportunity can complicate the intelligence processing, exploitation, and dissemination (PED) process because lower level units are not staffed to gather, analyze, store, and disseminate information that exists outside of traditional intelligence channels. Effective use of distributed units requires a concerted effort at the operational level to work through PED-related issues such as authorities, bandwidth, classification, and latency. Vulnerability to cyber attack or disruptions must be carefully considered as well. At the tactical level, units may require additional personnel such as foreign disclosure officers to support information processing or commercial networks to extend connectivity. Given appropriate capabilities and the means and authorities to employ them,

dispersed units can help the JFC to gain a more comprehensive, timely, and holistic appreciation for conditions in the JOA.

(4) Even when the JFC's mission focuses on one type of operation such as counterinsurgency, widely distributed units can have disparate information and intelligence requirements. These require a tailored approach to planning and collection from the joint force HQ down through tactical intelligence organizations and battalion intelligence sections. This situation can be complicated by the limited bandwidth available at small unit level to receive this information. A solution may be to push experienced intelligence personnel and tailored analytical capabilities down to dispersed units.

(5) Higher level requests for information may exhaust the small units' organic ISR capabilities. Distributed units may need to be reinforced with additional assets if high-tempo operations are anticipated and personnel and equipment are available. This too may become a management problem for the both the JFC and dispersed unit leaders. An option to mitigate this issue could be to establish elements of the national intelligence support team (NIST) at the component level or lower. While the NIST is doctrinally located at the JTF HQ, JFCs should consider establishing mini-NISTs at the senior component or lower level.

(6) There are a variety of means to enable components and tactical units to leverage ISR assets and information in the execution of their missions. These include providing a graphic presentation of the collection plan with collection asset, time, and collection target (e.g., ISR synchronization matrix) to the components and distributed units. Such a solution would require the units to have access to SIPRNET due to the classification of the information.

(7) The capability and capacity of higher echelons to receive and act on information passed from distributed units should be as robust as the capability to pass information down to these units. This may require providing improved communications links and processes and additional intelligence personnel to these units. A dedicated joint regional environmental information center would be a potentially useful tool to gather information, develop focused products, and improve dissemination of that information to all interested parties and authorized interorganizational partners.

(8) Intelligence must be available at the lowest appropriate classification. This is particularly important to ensure information gets to small and widely dispersed units and their interorganizational partners. When feasible, and within established disclosure guidelines, JFCs should consider an option of providing selected intelligence on a "need to share" basis rather than a strict "need to know" restriction.

4. Movement and Maneuver

a. The *movement and maneuver function* includes a number of tasks, such as deploying, shifting, regrouping, or moving joint or component force formations within the operations area by any means or mode (air, land, or sea). More specifically, *maneuver* is the employment of forces in the operations area through movement in combination with fires to achieve a position of advantage in respect to the enemy in order to accomplish the mission.[36]   Maneuver unit commanders seek to overwhelm the enemy with a near simultaneous array of pressing decisions with increasingly time-compressed windows. *Mission command* facilitates maneuver, since maneuver often occur in conjunction with engaging the enemy. In the heat of an engagement, leaders don't have the opportunity to stop their maneuver to ask for orders. Applied to widely dispersed operations, mission command enables the commander's effort by greatly expanding the number of subordinate decision makers empowered to exercise unique initiative in accord with common purpose. Their many unpredictable and perhaps seemingly discordant actions executed with speed and violence can induce cognitive overload, panic, and systemic shock that crack the coherence of enemy response. When receiving enemy action, mission command's decentralization of authority distributes the decision process among a wider array of decision makers who can withstand a similar flurry of action without losing their composure.

The "Chindits" in Distributed Operations, World War II

The **Chindits** (officially in 1943 the 77th Indian Infantry Brigade and in 1944 the 3rd Indian Infantry Division) were a British India "Special Force" that served in Burma and India in 1943 and 1944 during the Burma Campaign in World War II.   They were formed into long-range penetration groups trained to operate deep behind Japanese lines. Most of the members of the Chindits were from units of the British Army and Gurkha units of the British Indian Army. Personnel recruited in Burma served as reconnaissance troops. Some United States personnel were attached to the Chindits, or served in a US Army Air Force unit specifically formed to support the Chindits in the field.[37]

During the Second World War, in the China-Burma-India Theater, British and Indian "Chindits" employed long-range penetration tactics, in which numerous separated columns simultaneously infiltrated the Japanese Army's rear areas, in dispersed fashion. These units were large enough to inflict a heavy blow to the enemy, but small enough to avoid decisive engagement if outnumbered. Supplied by air and with close air support as a substitute for artillery, they would penetrate the jungle on foot, essentially relying on surprise through mobility to target enemy lines of communication (a tactic which the Japanese had previously been using to great effect in Singapore and in Burma in 1942 against British forces).   The columns operated behind Japanese lines for extended periods of time, forming concentrations, in some instances, to establish strong bastions astride Japanese lines of communications.[38]

---

[36] JP 1-02.

[37] http://en.wikipedia.org/wiki/Chindits. This paragraph is summarized from the Wikipedia article *Chindits,* which contains citations for primary sources.

[38] USMC *A Concept for Distributed Operations,* p. IV.

b. Once deployed to its area of operations, a unit's ability to maneuver depends on many factors such as its organic transportation and the nature of the terrain. Risk increases when the unit is beyond mutually supporting range of other friendly units, since security becomes a 360-degree requirement. "If they have no relative mobility advantage over enemy forces, dispersed forces are susceptible to flanking and the ever constricting geometry of enemy fire."[39] Following are examples of considerations related to the movement and maneuver function.

(1) A joint force's ground components have a variety of organic transportation capabilities that can support the movement, mobility, and maneuver of distributed units. In this handbook's scenario, JTF Blue's JFLCC would establish priorities for those assets under the JFLCC's control to support the approved CONOPS. These would typically include placing additional assets in a supporting relationship (or under TACON) of those units. The JFLCC should coordinate with the JFC and joint force J-4 for additional assets if necessary.

(2) The J-4 is responsible for advising the JTF commander of the logistic support that can be provided for proposed COAs and approved CONOPS. In general, the J-4 formulates policies for the JTF commander's approval to ensure effective logistic support for all forces in the command and coordinates execution of the commander's logistic policies and guidance.

(3) JFCs should plan for various ways and means to help maneuver forces attain positional advantage. For example, SOF may expose vulnerabilities through special reconnaissance and attack the enemy through direct action or unconventional warfare using indigenous or surrogate forces. Additionally, the use of information operations may minimize civilian interference with operations as well as the impact of military operations on the populace.

(4) A distributed unit's need for additional non-organic assets will depend on its mission, resources, and the nature of the threat. For example, an infantry battalion's mission in the JFC's COIN operation might focus on moving to and occupying an AO and protecting the local population in a region where insurgent activity has been limited. In this primarily defensive mission, the battalion commander might establish company AOs with platoons working from widely dispersed patrol bases that collectively provide coverage for the battalion's AO. Another battalion's mission in a large AO with significant insurgent activity might be to move to and through the area, clear the area of insurgents, and then occupy the area and protect the population. The largely offensive phase of this operation could require additional assets to support anticipated maneuver, particularly to engage insurgent targets of opportunity (such as a base) identified in the AO but far from the battalion's main effort.

(5) Initial force deployments to immature or undeveloped AOs will generate different planning considerations from those for more mature or developed AOs. The initial deployment of adequate joint capabilities is crucial, and commanders must appreciate that distributed operations will often require more non-organic support than other types of operations. The ability to maneuver or move, depending on the military activity, may be less difficult in the latter circumstance as road networks may be more expansive and transport platforms may be more available (in the form of prepositioned equipment, contractor procured, or host nation provided).

---

[39] Enhanced MAGTF Operations (EMO), MCCDC, page 8.

Since distributed operations may place additional transportation requirements on the JTF, this should be part of the analysis when determining the operational approach and the extent to which units will be dispersed. Commanders must always be alert to the dangers of deploying ground forces without sufficient joint and organic capabilities.[40]

(6) There can be competing demands for movement and maneuver resources from the joint force's interagency partners. A consistent theme in unit after-action reports from Iraq and Afghanistan and senior advisor observations is that early establishment of relationships with higher, adjacent, or supporting coalition member's transportation elements was key to mutual support, and that participation in training or exercises with these partners helps establish those relationships.

5. Fires

a. *Fires* are the use of weapon systems to create a specific lethal or nonlethal effect on a target.[41] Much has been done in the last few years to increase the effectiveness of supporting fires. Additional joint fire observers, improved communications, streamlined procedures, and forward-basing of air assets along with airborne alerts have increased the responsiveness of air support. JFCs have also decentralized many non-lethal fires such as electronic attack. However, at the JFC level, joint fires officers must continually assess the ability to provide responsive joint fires across the entire JOA including the areas between noncontiguous units.

Operation ANACONDA, Afghanistan

Operation Anaconda took place in early March 2002 in which the United States military and CIA Paramilitary Officers, working with allied Afghan military forces, and other NATO and non NATO forces attempted to destroy al-Qaeda and Taliban forces in the Shahi-Kot Valley and Arma Mountains southeast of Zormat. This operation was the first large-scale battle in the United States war in Afghanistan since the Battle of Tora Bora in December 2001. This was the first operation in the Afghanistan theater to involve a large number of U.S. conventional (i.e., non-Special Operations) forces participating in direct combat activities.[42]

In a National Defense University Lessons Learned report on Operation Anaconda, the assertion was made that joint doctrine "calls for a mutually supporting blend of ground, sea, and air-delivered fires." Operation Anaconda showed that, at a minimum, one of these types of fire support must be present in adequate amounts if another is lacking. This is especially important if the forces needing support are distributed. During

---

[40] The NDU Anaconda report operation report states, "In future battles, the idea of using distant fires to support dispersed ground forces could work only if great care is taken—in advance—to prepare fully for the operation. In other cases, this idea might not be viable at all if it is carried to the point of not equipping the ground forces with organic fires of their own…. Operation Anaconda suggests that the Army faces a challenge in ensuring that its light forces will be sufficiently well-armed and agile for such encounters." See Richard L. Kugler, Michael Baranick, and Hans Binnendijk, Operation Anaconda: Lessons for Joint Operations, National Defense University, March 2009, page xiii.

[41] JP 1-02

[42] http://en.wikipedia.org/wiki/Operation_Anaconda, which contains citations for primary sources.

Anaconda, US Army forces committed to battle found themselves unexpectedly isolated (unintentionally distributed) in the face of a determined enemy. The absence of Army artillery and additional mortars resulted from tactical mobility choices as well as shortage of helicopter lift support. The effect was to put increased pressure on the air component to deliver a higher volume of fires than originally anticipated. It also compelled the air component to overcome constraints to perform missions that may have been more easily performed by Army organic fires that were not available."[43] The report provides examples of constraints on supporting fires during this operation. These included proximity of friendly forces to the enemy, the need for simultaneous CAS missions during the battle, and the adverse effect of mountainous terrain on maneuver and both target identification and engagement.

b. Whenever combat is likely, ground force combat operations planning should include "…a mutually supporting blend of ground fires and air delivered fires."[44] Whether maneuvering in concert with other units and directly supported by centralized fires, or operating more independently, the latitude provided by mission orders enables more agile maneuver, faster response, and more dexterous action.

c. Following are considerations.

(1) The ability and responsibility of decentralized decision makers to coordinate fires and maneuver in all directions, both in terms of contiguous battle-space and organizational relationships, is critical to preparing for opportunity. Generally, there are four alternatives for increasing a dispersed unit's capability to employ fires.

o From a fires perspective, a unit is typically more self-reliant when it has more organic or attached firepower. Providing additional firepower through *attachment*[45] makes it immediately available to the unit commander, but it also increases sustainment requirements.

o Lateral self-coordination authority forward between and among maneuver and supporting forces can enable the timely, agile, and effective action (particularly fire support) necessary to exploit fleeting opportunity.

o Third, an alternative is to place non-organic fires capabilities, such as the component's artillery, in direct support of the distributed unit and to ensure that close air support is immediately available. But artillery might not be able to support all distributed units when they are dispersed across an extensive operations area. In that case, the component's attack helicopters may be able to supplement the JFACC's CAS.

o A fourth alternative is to give the unit commander control of capabilities normally controlled by the joint force or component HQ. With proper planning, unmanned aerial vehicles, such as fires-capable Predators (and the upgraded Warrior and Reaper variants), can provide

---

[43] Kugler, Baranick, and Binnendijk, page xii.

[44] Kugler, Baranick, and Binnendijk, page xii

[45] JP 1-02. *Attachment* is the relatively temporary placement of units or personnel with another unit to perform a specific function. In this instance, it requires a C2 relationship such as TACON.

"24/7" air support coverage for a distributed unit by means of a direct link between the unit commander and the UAV ground control station.

(2) How isolated a unit is from its normal support is a key consideration in determining the required extent, nature, and responsiveness of non-organic support. Operations in Iraq have shown that dedicated assets from various echelons to specific, subordinate units enabled these units to rapidly employ fires in response to a changing tactical situation. However, "dedicating" assets to one unit limits the flexibility to employ these assets elsewhere in the JOA.

(3) As ground units disperse over wider areas, control of air support becomes a critical issue. Commanders might consider pushing a capability similar to the USMC *direct air support center* capability, in the form of *air support liaison teams*, and some USAF element for airspace coordination down to the lowest appropriate level. Brigade and regiment-level teams (rather than the typical Service/functional component or division level) would be the likely candidate, with perhaps augmentation at battalion level as trained personnel become available and conditions warrant.

(4) Operational innovation in Iraq has provided procedures for integrating improved air support of dispersed forces. Preapproved "weaponeering" options and rehearsed battle drills can shorten engagement timelines for supporting air and surface fires in dense urban environments. These procedures include:

o   Tailored use of low collateral damage weapons engagements in densely populated areas.

o   Urban features and obstacles can be pre-measured, reducing coordination requirements during execution.

o   Rehearsed battle drills can facilitate rapid and effective engagement of the enemy.

o   Authorities for performing collateral damage estimation in accordance with ROE can be released to tactical levels provided they have the required training and tools to expedite fires.

o   Increased numbers of joint terminal attack controllers and joint fire observers at the small distributed unit.

o   Additional pre-coordinated procedures can quickly process immediate targets for attack. Procedures include kill boxes, planned targets, and missions integrated into the fire support plan.

(5) The need for specific, tailored ROE become increasingly important as units become more dispersed over a larger area, as authority for ordering and directing fires is pushed down to lower levels, and as non-military organizations proliferate within the AO.

(6) Various control measures, such as *airspace coordinating measures*, can limit the responsiveness of fires if execution procedures do not consider how to quickly overcome conflicting measures. The following observations concerning fires from a USMC company commander conducting operations in Afghanistan are instructive:

> "*Fire support became a civilian aircraft air clearance issue with the use of Excalibur rounds or HIMARS because their max ordnance (sic) went above the air space used by civilian aircraft. It was painful; not anything Marines could fix because the coordination was exceptionally high in the chain. It could take as long as 45 minutes in some cases; potentially too late to be of use.*"
>
> Company Commander
> (2/28th Brief), MCCLL Collection

6. Sustainment

a. *Sustainment* is the provision of logistics and personnel services required to maintain and prolong operations until successful mission accomplishment.[46] Sustainment is a significant challenge when units are widely dispersed as part of the operational approach because of the non-contiguous nature of the operating area and extended distances between units.

b. This section discusses sustainment risk, planning, and logistical considerations.

(1) The JFC must understand the logistical implications and risks of distributing forces widely throughout the JOA. Evaluation of risk and mitigating factors should be addressed early in the planning process. Logistics support must balance mission requirements and associated risks while providing the JFC with the necessary degree of freedom of action and operational flexibility. Examples of risk include sustainment of widely dispersed units, protecting logistics assets moving through or over contested routes or territory, limiting the number of distribution methods available to support dispersed forces, and providing critical casualty care to all units.

(2) The JFC must be aware that SOF operating in a dispersed environment have limited capacity to supply, maintain, and support forces during sustained operations. Some general purpose force enablers can also be used to maximize the operational effectiveness of SOF.

(3) The tendency among planners is to centralize logistics operations to increase efficiency. Even though centralization may have this effect, it can also reduce support effectiveness because responsiveness to widely separated units may decrease. To achieve an appropriate balance between effectiveness and efficiency, limited resources must be skillfully allocated, maintaining the capability to respond to unanticipated requirements and shifting threats.

---

[46] JP 1-02.

(4) While flexibility is a key component in all logistics planning, it is particularly crucial while supporting widely distributed forces. Logistics planners must consider a wide range of possible contingencies and avoid creating single points of failure. For example, United States Transportation Command (USTRANSCOM) and the Defense Logistics Agency (DLA), in coordination with the Joint Staff and the geographic combatant commands, began the development of what has come to be called the Northern Distribution Network (NDN). This network mitigates the risk of potential problems with the southern LOCs through Pakistan by providing LOCs into Afghanistan from the north.[47]

(5) Ownership, allocation, and synchronization of transportation and other assets contribute to the complexities of planning and executing logistics operations in a distributed environment. Each Service owns transportation assets and has established procedures for using them. "Support" relationships may be required to effectively utilize these assets.

(6) Planners should consider and plan for a broad range of conditions to ensure there is sufficient capability and flexibility to deliver critical classes of supply and medical capabilities. Though not all inclusive, some general *logistical considerations* are discussed below.

o Distribution Flexibility. Conducting operations in harsh or remote environments or where the infrastructure is immature may require innovative air and surface transportation solutions to sustain the force. Due to resource constraints, organic means may be insufficient to re-supply widely dispersed units. Commanders may have to rely on host nation support or contracted resources to deliver critical commodities such as fuel, food, ammunition, and repair parts.

> **Logistic Considerations**
>
> - Distribution Flexibility
> - Complex LOCs
> - Tailored Logistics Concepts
> - HN Contracting Support
> - Medical Services

✓ Limited port throughput, host nation support, contract lift support and overflight rights, as well as aircraft bed-down limitations, diplomatic clearance requirements, availability of tanker assets, and other factors may complicate the deployment planning and impede or delay force closure. These considerations are especially important when operations involve deployment of forces through or over international borders or in multiple countries.

✓ Where there are immature or non-existing aerial ports of debarkation or seaport of debarkation, the JFC should consider using JTF Port Opening (JTF-PO) to facilitate operations. JTF-PO provides rapidly accessible capability for sea and airport offload and initial distribution capability.

---

[47] https://www.navsup.navy.mil/scnewsletter/2009/may-june/cover4

Operation UNIFIED RESPONSE, Haiti

In Operation Unified Response in Haiti, Airmen from the 621st Contingency Response Wing based at Joint Base McGuire-Dix-Lakehurst, NJ arrived in Port-au-Prince, Haiti, just two days after the 7.0 earthquake devastated the island nation. They joined with the 688th Rapid Port Opening Element out of Fort Eustis, VA., to execute a JTF PO mission. This is the first time a JTF-PO was used in an actual disaster operation.[48]

✓ The JFC should plan for use of multiple delivery platforms. Emerging delivery options such as Joint Precision Air Drop System (JPADS), Low cost/low altitude aerial resupply and cargo unmanned aerial system (UAS) can be used for delivery of critical supplies to units in austere locations or when LOCs are vulnerable to attack or in the event of other disruption such as weather. See Figure III-5.

✓

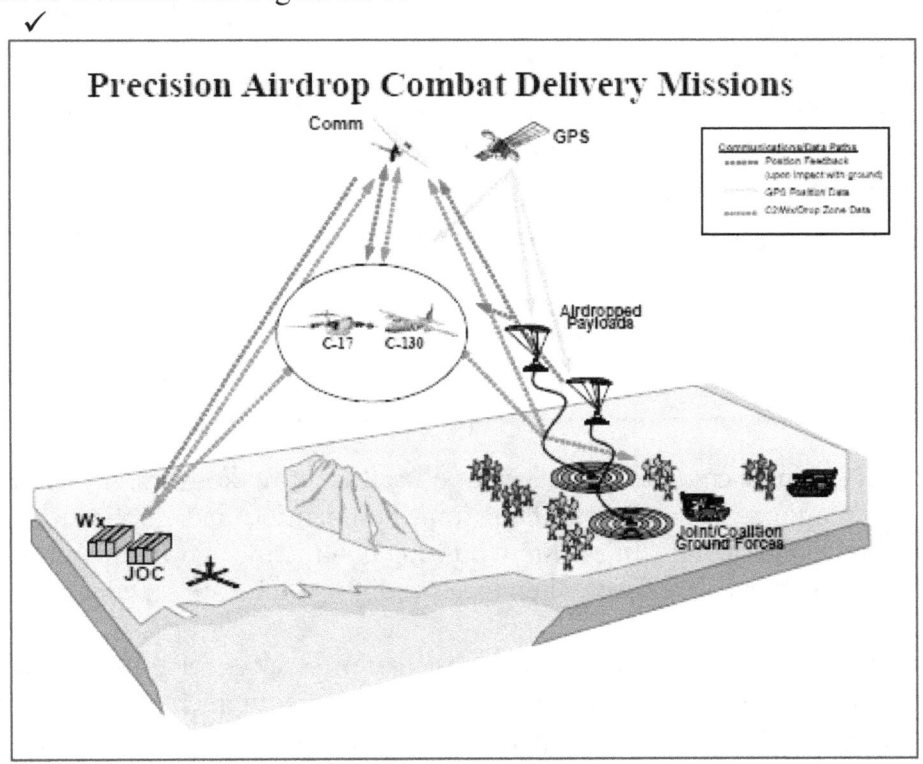

Figure III-5. Precision Airdrop Combat Delivery Missions

o Complex LOCs. Distances, terrain, degraded or non-existent transportation infrastructure, and likelihood of enemy action are all considerations that contribute to LOC challenges and security. LOC protection requirements may be extensive and affect multiple organizations. Organizations within the distribution pipeline must be provided with self-protection training and possess some level of embedded force protection capabilities. Additional discussion on protection is provided in the discussion of the *protection* function (see discussion in paragraph 7, "Protection."

---

[48] http://www.af.mil/news/story.asp?id=123189761

o <u>Tailored Logistics Concepts</u>. Formal links with DLA will enable logisticians to employ tailored logistics concepts such as kitting, pure package/pure pallet, and deployable depots. These concepts allow products to be packaged to meet the precise needs of the end user. Examples of kitting include Class VIII medical push packages and packages of preplanned and preconfigured essential logistics items (such as vehicle preventive maintenance kits). The deployable depots provide a scalable distribution operation that can receive, store, issue, and ship items to the end user. The depot also can provide tailored packages for small dispersed units and aid in synchronizing HN support.

o <u>HN Contracting Support</u>. When using host nation contractors, consider the resources available, ability of host nation vendors to fulfill contractual requirements, and the security environment. The following observations about contracting from a logistics officer supporting operations in Afghanistan are instructive:

> *"The issues we had with some of the contracts were that there wasn't much input from our level WRT (with regard to) determining requirements...so sometimes we had contracts for stuff that we couldn't necessarily use...One important consideration was trying to tie in some sort of escort for the contractor security without compromising your operational security."*
>
> **Logistics Officer (2/28th Brief), MCCLL Collection**
> **2nd Battalion, 8th Marines, Unit Debrief**

✓ A joint contracting cell can be used to provide oversight and a capability to synchronize contracting. This cell can help limit competition and duplication of contracting efforts amongst the components. In addition, pushing contracting and funding to small-unit level allows the units to get what they need, when they need it while helping the local economy.

✓ Dependence on contracted host nation support for critical functions conveys operational risk because of the lack of in-transit visibility of equipment or supplies being moved, unreliability in terms of schedule or capabilities actually provided, and the level of security. Also, availability of HN support may be limited due to a variety of factors that include domestic needs, competing demands from other claimants, and infrastructure damage resulting from hostile actions or natural events. Commanders should consider the use of contracted transportation for less sensitive, non-critical cargo, while bearing in mind these items will be at increased risk of loss, pilferage, or destruction by enemy action. Whenever possible, critical or sensitive items such as weapons, communications or security equipment, and ammunition should be transported and delivered using organic means.

✓ HN contracting may reduce the transportation requirements, stimulate the local economy and reduce the logistics footprint.

✓ HN contracting may also enable the distributed units to increase their self-sufficiency.

(7) Medical Services. Medical risks for distributed units should be carefully considered and explicitly addressed in command guidance and throughout the planning process. Widely dispersed operations place a premium on responsive medical treatment and evacuation needs. Allocation and apportionment of medical treatment and evacuation resources dictate that the joint force plans for the most advantageous locations of medical treatment facilities. It also requires coordination with components for overlapping evacuation areas of responsibility and reassessment of risk factors based on changes in the operational environment.

o The JFC should understand the potential effect that provision of medical care will have upon local and/or national medical infrastructure. During earthquake relief efforts in Pakistan, the US provided a high a level of medical care, unintentionally undercutting the local medical professionals and pharmacies.

o Commanders should also consider pushing additional medical personnel (such as independent duty corpsmen or physician assistant's) and medical evacuation capabilities (wheeled and air) forward with the distributed unit to increase the capabilities for care at the point of injury.

(8) The following comment from a commander in Afghanistan and the best practice that follows underscore the advantage of carefully managing and positioning medical capabilities forward during dispersed operations:

> "*Medical response can sometimes take more than an hour even by helicopter. Pushing medical assets forward on the battlefield is critical in this environment.*" ... "*Terrain and weather had a big impact on us. For example, in the mountains, fog and snow prevent use of aircraft, including MEDEVAC and CAS. Frequently, CAS was cancelled due to lack of ability to observe the ground or to navigate through the mountains.*"
>
> **Afghan Commander AAR Book, OEF 7**

(9) *Observed Best Practice:* The Marine Corps Shock Trauma Platoon is an example of an option that can mitigate the distributed unit's increased distance from medical treatment facilities. This platoon is self-contained and has a mobile medical unit composed of emergency medicine physicians, physician assistants, nurse, corpsmen and medically trained Marines. It has sufficient medical equipment to support 50 patients.

7. Protection

a. *Protection* is the preservation of the effectiveness and survivability of mission-related military and nonmilitary personnel, equipment, facilities, information, and infrastructure deployed or located within or outside the boundaries of a given operations area.[49] Per JP 3-0, protection focuses on conserving the joint force's fighting potential in four primary ways: active defensive measures, passive defensive measures, applying technology and procedures to reduce the risk of fratricide, and emergency management and response.

b. The non-contiguous and widely dispersed nature of distributed operations tends to create additional protection issues. The JFC can address many of these issues by employing control mechanisms and processes identified in JP 3-10, *Joint Security Operations in Theater*. The more difficult issue at the joint force and primary component levels will be identifying and allocating resources to address force protection risks and vulnerabilities identified by the distributed units. As with the other joint functions, the limiting factor may be the availability and responsiveness of capabilities needed to adequately protect the force and the mission.

(1) Protection is not limited to just the joint force. The JFC may be required to protect interorganizational partners or the local population in areas where other protection resources may be very limited. However, protection is a shared responsibility and must be coordinated with all stakeholders.

(2) To mitigate some of the risk to distributed forces in noncontiguous operations areas, consider implementation of control mechanisms and procedures outlined in JP 3-10, *Joint Security Operations in Theater*. These include establishing joint security areas (JSA) and conducting joint security operations (JSO), and have proven to be effective during operations in Iraq and Afghanistan. Joint security coordination centers and movement control centers also enhance security.

o A JSA is a specific surface area, designated by the JFC to facilitate protection of joint bases and their connecting lines of communications that support joint operations.[50]

o JSO provide for the defense of the joint force and facilitate force protection actions in designated areas. JSA and JSO provide for unity of effort and efficient use of constrained resources to maintain a relatively secure environment allowing the JFC to focus on the primary mission. JSO may entail the participation of host nation or coalition forces. The JFC will establish the operational framework that best addresses the operational environment while providing for maximum flexibility.

o The establishment of a joint security coordination center (JSCC) using elements from the JFC staff and representatives from all components operating in the operations area will also assist in meeting joint security requirements.

---

[49] JP 1-02.
[50] JP 1-02.

---

o   The establishment of a joint movement center (JMC). The JMC executes movement control and coordination of convoys passing through higher-level organizational and cross-Service boundaries. JSCC links to the JMC helps to support LOC security efforts throughout the operations area. One viable technique to link the JSC and JMC planning functions is to establish a joint LOC security board.

(3) Dispersed units are inherently more vulnerable. These units will, as a matter of routine, require greater protection resources such as barrier materials. This is an operational as well as a logistics issue.

(4) The greatest risk to distributed operations may be the threat to supply routes. Some LOC protection considerations include:

o   Planning to provide and protect sustainment and movement activities should begin at inception, not as an informal process after operations have begun.

o   Consider movement along the LOCs as an integral part of the scheme of maneuver. At the JTF and component level, this perspective will help to keep an operational focus on movements across the LOCs.

(5) The size of the JOA and various factors will cause air and missile defense organizations to face the same challenges as close air support. Component commanders can augment the most vulnerable units with additional short-range air defense systems. A large JOA will challenge effective placement of medium-range air defense systems.

US Marines in Distributed Operations, Vietnam[51]

Drawing from previous experience in "small wars," the United States Marine Corps employed a rudimentary form of distributed operations, known as the Combined Action Program during the Vietnam War from 1965 to 1971. "The Combined Action Platoon's (CAP) genesis was not a deliberate plan from higher headquarters; rather, it was a solution of one infantry battalion's problem of an expanding Tactical Area of Responsibility (TAOR). The concept of combining a squad of Marines with local Popular Forces (PF) and assigning them a village to protect proved to be a force multiplier. The CAP concept was effective in denying the enemy a sanctuary at the local village level.

The Pacification campaign seemed to work under the CAP concept, and the Marines fully embraced it. The approach involved squad-sized Marine units deployed in villages, fighting alongside Vietnamese Popular Force militia.

---

[51] Brewington, Brooks R., "Combined Action Platoons: A Strategy for Peace Enforcement." The highlighted vignette is extracted from parts of Maj Brewington's paper developed for the 1996 Marine Corps Command and Staff Course.

Combined Action Platoons worked in coordination with conventional Marine forces that possessed greater mobility and combat power. The CAP's were under the operational control of a Combined Action Company (CAC). A Marine captain was the company commander and was located at the District Headquarters where he had three or four Marines to assist him. His primary duties were to maintain radio contact with the CAP's, establish liaison with the District chief, and make periodic checks to each CAP site. The company commander was usually so far away that he personally could not react immediately to a CAP's call for reinforcement but rather show up the next day to assess the damage. CAP reinforcement came from other CAP's or mainline units in the area. Radio communicators were key to CAP survival in emergencies.

Area of Operations of CAP 2-7-4

In the Combined Action Program, separation and interdependent tactical actions were effective within an operational framework designed for area stability and counterinsurgency. Objectively, there is no solid proof that the CAP concept was a resounding success; however, subjectively the evidence suggests otherwise."

CHAPTER IV
OPERATIONAL IMPLICATIONS

"U.S. military power today is unsurpassed on the land and sea and in the air, space, and cyberspace. The individual Services have evolved capabilities and competencies to maximize their effectiveness in their respective domains. Even more important, the ability to integrate these diverse capabilities into a joint whole that is greater than the sum of the Service parts is an unassailable American strategic advantage."

**Admiral M.G. Mullen
Chairman of the Joint Chiefs of Staff
Capstone Concept for Joint Operations, January 2009**

1. Introduction

a. Operating with forces distributed beyond mutually supporting range has always posed challenges. These have been mitigated to some extent over time by improvements related to the areas of **d**octrine, **o**rganization, **t**raining, **m**ateriel, **l**eadership and education, **p**ersonnel, and **f**acilities (DOTMLPF).[52] However, there is significant room for improvement in some of these areas. The following statement from the CCJO is relevant:

> *"**Create agile general-purpose forces capable of operating independently at increasingly lower echelons.** This concept suggests the imperative for general-purpose forces increasingly to possess attributes commonly associated with special operations forces. These attributes include agility, speed of command and control, cultural sensitivity, the aptitude for highly discriminate action, and the ability to operate independently at lower echelons while possessing the access to a wide array of support."[53]*

b. As the joint force leverages distributed operations either by design or necessity, the joint community must invest in DOTMLPF solutions that reduce the risk inherent in widely dispersed employment of forces and provide additional capabilities to these units as required to accomplish their mission. The following paragraphs describe operational implications in each of the DOTMLPF areas (except in the facilities area, which has no identified implications).

---

[52] This model exists to support the *Joint Capabilities Integration and Development System.* See CJCSI 3170.01G.

[53] Capstone Concept for Joint Operations, p. 31.

2. Doctrine

a. As this handbook describes, the dispersed units in question typically are those of the joint force land components. Therefore, Army and Marine Corps capstone doctrine should address planning and execution considerations related to how their organizations will conduct and support distributed operations. Lower-level Service manuals can expand on capstone doctrine to provide the detailed considerations, tactics, techniques, and procedures relevant to conducting these operations. Service manuals also should address how higher-level Service and/or functional component HQ will push additional Service-controlled capabilities down to lower-level dispersed units.

b. Joint doctrine should address planning considerations related to supporting the joint force Service component (or functional component when formed) with joint capabilities beyond those the component can provide. The JFC and component commanders should initially identify possible requirements early in operational design as the commanders collaborate while developing the operational approach (see Chapter II, *Operational Design and Planning*). One issue that doctrine (or the joint force standing operating procedures) must address is interaction between the joint force element that typically controls a specific capability and the low-level Service unit that will control it during operations. For example, if a tactical air control party is not available to the ground unit commander, can the typical company commander or platoon leader receive UAV-based fire support by talking directly with the UAV controller regardless of the controller's geographical location?

c. Depending on the operational environment and nature of the mission, a dispersed unit may require support related to all joint functions. Joint doctrine publications should be revised as necessary to address support to distributed operations. Examples include the following:

(1) JP 3-0, *Joint Operations*, should acknowledge the potential for support to distributed operations in the chapter that discusses joint functions.

(2) JP 5-0, *Joint Operation Planning*, should address operational design and planning considerations.

(3) The JP 2-0, *Joint Intelligence*, and relevant subordinate intelligence publications should address intelligence preparation of the operational environment and specific intelligence support. Key publications in the JP 2 series include JP 2-01, *Joint and National Intelligence Support to Joint Operations;* JP 2-01.2, *Counterintelligence and Human Intelligence in Joint Operations;* and JP 2-01.3, *Joint Intelligence Preparation of the Operational Environment.*

(4) Key publications in the JP 3-0 series include JP 3-01, *Countering Air and Missile Threats*; JP 3-05.1, *Joint Special Operations Task Force Operations*; JP 3-09, *Joint Fire Support*; JP 3-09.3, *Close Air Support (CAS)*; and JP 3-24, *Counterinsurgency Operations*; and JPs 3-30, 3-31, and 3-32, which cover C2 of joint air, land, and maritime operations respectively. Many other JP 3-0 series publications are relevant.

(5) Key publications in the JP 4-0 series (*Joint Logistics*) include JP 4-02, *Health Service Support*; JP 4-09, *Distribution Operations*; and JP 4-10, *Operational Contract Support*.

(6) JP 6-0, *Joint Communications System*, should expand the discussion on the joint aerial layered network and could identify specific communications capabilities that could supplement those organic to dispersed ground units.

3. Organization

a. Joint and Service component headquarters are typically robust enough to control unique aspects of support to distributed operations across the six joint functions. However, battalions have less capability to do so. Company commanders, who might often be the recipient of additional capabilities described in this handbook, will be challenged to operate in a dispersed combat environment and effectively employ the additional capabilities made available.

b. Services should determine organizational adjustments to companies and battalions that might facilitate operating in a distributed manner and controlling capabilities pushed down from higher component and joint headquarters. These might be temporary adjustments that would occur as operations begin, or they could be permanent changes to the organization's tables of organization and equipment.

c. The joint community should determine the form in which a joint force or supporting joint organization will provide capabilities to subordinate units. In other words, will a hardware, software, or other system be provided for use by the distributed unit's operators (problematic at and below company level), or will the system come as a package with operators, transportation, and other required support. **The employment philosophy should be one of enabling the supported unit without encumbering it with additional support requirements**.

4. Training

a. Training for support to distributed ground operations should be balanced between time spent on joint, individual, unit, and leader training during pre-deployment, deployment, and post-deployment training periods. Joint considerations related to these operations should be included in joint training events and instruction by training elements such as US Joint Forces Command deployable joint training teams.

> *"Thanks to advances in areas ranging from communications and information sharing to munitions effectiveness, it increasingly is becoming possible to achieve joint synergy at lower echelons of command without incurring the risks and inefficiencies associated with piecemealing the assets themselves. Thus, in the future, the chief prerequisites for the continued devolution of joint synergy downward will have to do with cross-Service education and training and the continued development of more flexible and adaptable joint planning and coordination mechanisms -- all of which help to lower the inherent costs of joint integration."* [54]

---

[54] *Capstone Concept for Joint Operations*, p. 25.

b. Training on how to support distributed operations should be conducted for any Service or joint processes, systems, and organizations that are planned to be provided to affected units. Whether this training is joint or Service-provided will depend on who owns the specific capability. Both Service and joint training should encompass relevant aspects of operations with interorganizational partners, since their support to isolated units could be essential to mission accomplishment.

5. Materiel

a. Multi-mission platforms, which can provide support across two or more joint functions, deserve greater investment. Expanded operating areas and units that are separated by great distances must have the ability to stay connected to a variety of networks and will have to be sustained and maintained in a more independent manner.

b. Services should consider whether certain systems, once retained only to support higher headquarters, could be included in the future as part of company or battalion tables of organization and equipment.

c. Development of a robust joint aerial layered network (JALN) will require joint and Service investments.

6. Leadership and Education

a. This is one of the most important capability development efforts for both small unit leaders executing distributed operations and for senior leaders providing the Service component and joint capabilities and support. In general, the focus of leader development efforts should remain consistent with the current trend of developing innovative and adaptive leaders who can respond effectively to a wide variety of circumstances.

b. Current programs serve joint and Service forces well as they deal with the complexities of today's operational environment. However, operating in combat and widely isolated from other units places a premium on expertise, confidence, decisiveness, and other attributes required to act in the absence of guidance beyond the original plan. Key to this ability is *mission command — the conduct of military operations through decentralized execution based upon mission-type orders* (see discussion in Chapter III). Commanders and other leaders from joint force down to squad level must understand the philosophy and practice of mission command, and this should be a topic of emphasis during joint and Service education as well as training.

c. Pushing responsibility and authority to increasingly lower levels requires trust and confidence between leaders and subordinates. How leaders manage risk, provide commander's guidance and commander's intent, and "visualize the operational environment" is both an art and science that the Services must address more directly and earlier in the development of commissioned and non-commissioned leaders. The Services are ultimately responsible for developing their senior and junior leaders, but the following ideas could be helpful from a joint perspective. Specifically:

(1) Pursue greater participation by interagency personnel in professional military education schools.

(2) Facilitate knowledge sharing and development of adaptability-related skills.

(3) Incorporate decision-making exercises (DMXs) in educational and training environments to develop adaptability-related skills.

(4) Develop a robust red-teaming structure with online and mobile training teams capable of supporting DMXs in the live training environment. The red-team support structure should be capable of simultaneously providing adaptable, capabilities-based adversaries to multiple DMXs at the strategic, operational, and tactical levels.

(5) Enhance the Small Unit of Excellence concept of small-unit immersion training by including more operational and strategic considerations and to facilitate learning adaptability.

7. Personnel

The training, leadership, and education paragraphs have addressed important initiatives related to personnel. However, the most difficult challenge for the Services might be one of recruiting, screening, and selecting junior leaders who can handle the increased responsibility and authority common in distributed operations. Certain personal attributes essential to such operations are inherent in the individual. If these attributes exist, innovative education can enhance them. Services' selection and advancement processes could require adjustment to identify and groom individuals who posses these attributes.

This Page Intentionally Blank

CHAPTER V
CONCLUSION

"Dispersed fighting, whether the dispersal is caused by the terrain, the lack of supplies, or by the skills of the enemy, will have two main requirements—skilled and determined junior leaders and self-reliant, physically hard, well-disciplined troops. Success in future land operations will depend on the immediate availability of such leaders and such soldiers, ready to operate in small independent formations."[55]

Field-Marshal Viscount Slim
Commander, British XIVth Army
Defeat Into Victory

1. This handbook is a pre-doctrinal document intended to stimulate thinking about how the joint force and component commanders can plan for and provide capabilities to tactical units, principally battalion level and below, which better enable these units to operate in a distributed manner. The handbook, while not authoritative, serves as a bridge between current best practices in the field and the potential incorporation of value-added ideas in joint doctrine. This concluding chapter highlights the key ideas presented in previous chapters.

2. It is instructive to revisit the description of distributed operations established in Chapter I, and recall the relevance of the phrase "…beyond mutually supporting range" (see paragraph 2d in Chapter I). The importance of the distributed operations construct is not in how to disperse and support units performing relatively safe activities associated with engagement, relief, and reconstruction, even though dispersed circumstances will cause some of the same sustainment and communications challenges. **The importance of the construct resides instead in supporting units that face dangerous circumstances involving combat when they cannot support each other and when response across the joint functions must be quick and effective.**

3. There are three primary reasons for widely dispersing forces in combat. **One** is when friendly forces face a numerically superior enemy in situations when friendly forces do not have dimensional superiority (such as air superiority). **Another** is when the commander expects the enemy to use weapons of mass destruction (particularly nuclear). These reasons are based largely on Cold War concerns, and could be relevant at some point in the future; but they are not typical of the current operational environment and are not addressed in this handbook.

4. This handbook focuses on the **third reason** for distributing forces — **because the commander determines it is the best way to accomplish the mission in spite of the inherent disadvantages of this approach.** The commander typically bases this decision on an understanding of the operational environment and the problem that must be solved as determined

---

[55] Slim, pp. 549-550.

during operational design and planning. Despite potential disadvantages, there are compensating positive effects of dispersing units throughout the operations area, including the following:

a. Widely distributed units help increase the joint force's situational awareness and can provide an additional source of human intelligence.

b. These units can increase the joint force's influence among the population sooner, and can better ensure continuity of the higher commander's communication strategy themes and messages than if the units were centrally located.

c. A distributed approach can restrict operations of an elusive irregular adversary by limiting or eliminating potential sanctuaries.

d. A distributed approach allows for concurrent rather than sequential or incremental operations throughout the area.

5. The inherent disadvantages in distributing small units (battalions, companies, and platoons) widely throughout a large operations area include the following:

a. The combat risk for these units increases. Because they are beyond the mutual support of like-type units, they must rely on limited organic capabilities, non-organic capabilities under their control, and/or responsive support from their Service component HQ and other joint force components.

b. Unit operations areas are typically noncontiguous; gaps between these areas can be harder to cover.

c. Command, control, and sustainment are more difficult. Terrain, distances, and enemy actions complicate and impede the joint force response in all six joint functional areas.

d. The stress on small unit leaders increases. In particular, relatively new company commanders and platoon leaders who have not experienced this situation before will face unfamiliar circumstances in a hostile environment for which current junior leader training programs do not currently prepare them.

6. Experience, lessons learned, and observed "best practices" during the past few years have demonstrated that the joint force can do more if the JFC and component commanders are willing to take measured risk with the dispersion of the force. But achieving "more" requires the following from commanders and staff alike:

a. Understanding the philosophy and practice of *mission command* — the conduct of military operations through decentralized execution based upon mission-type orders.

b. Accepting the discomfort of decentralizing operations and trusting subordinates.

c. Conducting collaborative, inclusive planning to the greatest extent possible, including every stakeholder who can influence the effectiveness of widely distributed units; making information-sharing an imperative.

d. Providing network connectivity that supports the extended operations areas common to distributed operations; developing "artful" solutions to use technology to create multi-tiered networks that optimize land, space, and aerial nodes.

e. Managing joint and component resources in a manner that pushes capabilities down to the lowest level where they can be integrated effectively in ongoing operations.

f. Recognizing that pushing capabilities lower means more than providing platforms; it means getting the right people, processes, systems and authorities down to the right level.

g. Underwriting the mistakes of their subordinate leaders, whereby senior leaders create a climate of innovation, adaptation and willingness by all to take calculated risks.

7. Distributed operations are not new. What may be new is the degree to which joint force and component commanders commit to distributed employment in the future, supported by development of relevant capabilities and risk-reduction measures. Ideally this commitment will be by choice. However, as we have learned repeatedly, the enemy gets a vote. Leaders at every level, but especially at the joint force and senior component level, must become expert at thinking through the merits and downsides of operating in a widely dispersed manner. Moreover, the doctrine, training, and other initiatives mentioned in the Chapter IV, *Operational Implications*, are necessary to fully enable the junior leaders who operate on the forward edge of distributed employment.

This Page Intentionally Blank

APPENDIX A

CONCEPT DEVELOPMENT AND EXPERIMENTATION

*"**Distributed Operations** describes an operating approach that requires new ways to educate and train our Marines and that guides us in the use of emerging technologies."*[56]

General M. W. Hagee
33rd Commandant of the Marine Corps

"Conventional wisdom tells us that the battalion is the smallest formation capable of sustained independent operations; current operations tell us it is the company."[57]

General James T. Conway
34th Commandant of the Marine Corps

" We will better educate and train our Marines to succeed in distributed operations and increasingly complex environments."[58]

General James F. Amos
35th Commandant of the Marine Corps

1. The Marine Corps and Distributed Operations

a. In April 2005, General M. W. Hagee, then Commandant of the Marine Corps, released the white paper entitled *A Concept for Distributed Operations*, which was "…intended to promote discussion and to generate ideas for specific combat development initiatives…," enabling small units to function with greater operational initiative and independence. Although forces have conducted operations in a distributed manner for various purposes throughout history, the Marine Corps 2005 paper could be considered the impetus for current joint efforts to describe these operations and determine how to support them. A 2008 Marine Corps paper, *A Concept for Enhanced Company Operations*, promotes the premise that even company-sized units must be able to conduct sustained, independent operations. The premise relies on units that have increased access to (and organic control of) functional support, whether from new capabilities made organic to the units or from capabilities provided by higher echelons. Both concepts intend to meet the challenges of current and anticipated operational environments by improving the

---

[56] Department of the Navy, Headquarters U.S. Marine Corps, *A Concept for Distributed Operations*, 25 April 2005. The referenced quote is in the concept's cover memorandum.

[57] Department of the Navy, Headquarters U.S. Marine Corps, *A Concept for Enhanced Company Operations*, 28 August 2008. The referenced quote is in the concept's cover memorandum.

[58] Department of the Navy, Headquarters U.S. Marine Corps, 35th Commandant of the Marine Corps, Commandant's Planning Guidance, 2010, p. 8. This statement is one of the Commandant's top four priorities.

Marine Corps' ability to conduct decentralized, small-unit operations in expeditionary warfare circumstances. The 2008 concept built on the results of experimentation and capability development to provide battalion commanders a critical link between operational planning and squad-level tactical execution.

> "*The essence of this concept lies in the capacity for coordinated action by dispersed units, throughout the breadth and depth of the battlespace, ordered and connected with an operational design focused on a common aim.*"
>
> **A Concept for Enhanced Company Operations**

b. In the Marine Corps' *distributed operations* concept, dispersed squads and platoons control large areas by coordinated tactical actions. They acquire intelligence, surveillance, and reconnaissance (ISR) sensor data directly or from external sensors while calling on external firepower and reliable long-range resupply. With small units (vs. battalions) given tactical initiative, their leaders' situation-awareness requirement becomes a significant challenge, as does squads' radio connectivity and casualty care. Dispersed units may have to move more equipment greater distances, worsening current individual overloads. As a result, their resupply and maintenance requirements may be increased sharply compared to those of non-dispersed units, yet current air and surface resupply are inadequate for real-time precision delivery at longer range.

c. In late 2005, Lieutenant General James N. Mattis, Commanding General of Marine Corps Combat Development Command (MCCDC), requested that the Naval Research Advisory Committee (NRAC) devote one of its annual Summer Studies to distributed operations by comparing and contrasting the emerging concept with conventional operations, determining how selected technology insertions could enable distributed operations, estimating risks associated with various options, and identifying potential show-stoppers. Lieutenant General Mattis' vision was that distributed operations would "unleash the combat power of the young Marine," and his guidance was for NRAC to focus on the "squad level as a system."[59] NRAC's top-level recommendations stated that the Marine Corps should:[60]

- Establish a "DO Marine as a System" Science & Technology (S&T) Program, resourced at approximately $50M/year for the level of challenge represented by DO as a transformational concept of operations.

- Ensure that communications and networking requirements of DO will be supported in planned DOD battle space architecture.

- Evaluate the feasibility, desirability, and means of aging the force in order to maximize return on investment in much more highly trained infantrymen.

- Retain or establish an "honest broker" (independent of vendors and integrators) to conduct DO communications system engineering.

---

[59] Naval Research Advisory Committee Report, *Distributed Operations*, July 2006, p.3.
[60] Ibid., p. 4.

2. Related Joint Initiatives

a. A distributed operations construct was first mentioned from a joint perspective in the October 2003 *Joint Operations Concepts* document, which stated, "To accomplish assigned missions, an adaptive joint force will be capable of conducting rapidly executable, globally and operationally distributed,[61] simultaneous and sequential operations."[62] "By integrating joint capabilities at increasingly lower echelons and enhancing connectivity among the elements, joint forces can better conduct distributed operations."[63]

b. In 2006, the *Major Combat Operations* (MCO) joint operating concept (JOC) addressed distributed operations in more detail by characterizing the construct as the **operating approach** to conducting MCO.[64] The concept stated that a JFC could, through distributed operations, achieve objectives when enabled with advanced capabilities in battlespace surveillance, strategic-to-tactical mobility, and comprehensive connectivity among key elements of the joint force. These capabilities would enable the joint force with the means to attack directly at the enemy's centers of gravity (COGs) from multiple directions. Simultaneously, the joint force would be able to see and protect against enemy attacks on the JFC's own COGs.[65] The MCO concept stated that distributed operations, "...describe an operational approach that creates an advantage over an adversary through the deliberate use of separate, coordinated and interdependent actions. Distributed operations are enabled by improved access to functional support, as well as by enhanced combat capabilities at tactical levels."[66] The concept also suggested that physically distributed joint forces would be "...virtually contiguous through a net-centric battlespace."[67]

c. The most recent approved joint concept, the Chairman of the Joint Chiefs of Staff 2009 *Capstone Concept for Joint Operations*, does not mention distributed operations per se. It focuses instead on a central operations thesis that revolves around the relationship and interaction of four "**categories of military activities**" — *combat*, *security*, *engagement*, and *relief and reconstruction*.[68] However, one of the CCJO's ten "**common operating precepts**" is instrumental to the success of operations by widely dispersed units, particularly of the ground components: "***Drive synergy to the lowest echelon at which it can be managed effectively.***"[69]

---

[61] Department of Defense, *Joint Operations Concepts*, JCS Version 1.0, 3 October 2003, p. 10. A footnote on page 10 of the DOD paper characterizes "distributed" as, "Forces, potentially geographically separated, sharing a common operational picture through a global network to enable the operational control of tempo and momentum to achieve the effects desired."

[62] Ibid., p. 10.

[63] Ibid., p. 15.

[64] Department of Defense, *Major Combat Operations Version 2.0* Joint Operating Concept, December 2006, p. 11. See Figure 6.

[65] Ibid., p. 14.

[66] *Major Combat Operations* JOC, p. 15.

[67] Ibid., p. 17.

[68] Department of Defense, *Capstone Concept for Joint Operations*, Version 3.0, 15 January 2009, p. 13.

[69] Ibid., p. 25. This precept has been incorporated in the Final Coordination draft of Joint Publication 3-0, *Joint Operations*.

(1) This precept acknowledges that the future operating environment will demand applying military power in ever-smaller increments, which in turn will require achieving joint synergy at ever-lower echelons of command. Joint integration that was once achieved at the component level or slightly below will be achieved routinely in the future at drastically lower echelons — even down to the small-unit level.

(2) Advances in areas ranging from communications and information sharing to munitions effectiveness increase the possibility of achieving joint synergy at lower echelons of command when widely distributed operations are necessary to mission accomplishment. **In practice, this can be interpreted as small unit control and use of joint capabilities that have been typically controlled by the joint force or its primary component headquarters'.**

d. The most recent joint initiative has been USJFCOM's draft *Joint Distributed Operations* (JDO) concept paper, related experimentation and reports, and this handbook. Concept development began in early 2009 with a purpose of informing experimentation on (and analysis and observation of) potential methods and capabilities for future joint initiatives, both within US Joint Forces Command and elsewhere.[70] The draft concept paper described JDO as follows:

> *"Joint distributed operations are joint operations characterized by forces widely dispersed in multiple domains throughout an operational area, often beyond mutually supporting range and operating independently of one another because of distance or differing missions or capabilities, but supported by a variety of nonorganic capabilities. The size of these distributed units will vary with the situation, but the idea is that these are formations traditionally not expected to be operationally self-sufficient for extended durations. These distributed elements will require support from other assets under the control of the joint force commander. **Therefore, the defining attributes of joint distributed operations are the dispersal of joint force elements throughout the operational area and the extensive use of non-organic capabilities to support them.**"* (emphasis added)

e. USJFCOM J9 examined the JDO concept in a series of six experiments and other events during the course of this initiative. A particularly noteworthy event was the 13-15 April 2010 Leader Seminar, which involved operationally-experienced leaders at the general officer/flag officer and field grade officer levels, with the support of Service and combatant command representatives, multinational partners, and subject matter experts. The Leadership Seminar final report contains details of the event and conclusions.[71] Chapter III of this handbook highlights key findings of this seminar, other experimentation, and insights from past and current operations.

---

[70] US Joint Forces Command, A Concept for Joint Distributed Operations, draft version 0.6.3, 11 November 2009, p. 3.

[71] Throughout the JDO experiment and development of the Handbook, general consensus was that there is no requirement for a new joint term or category for operations involving distributed forces; however, there was convergence of opinion on many of the concepts and ideas outlined in this handbook.

GLOSSARY

PART I — ABBREVIATIONS AND ACRONYMS

AO	area of operations
AOR	area of responsibility
C2	command and control
CAS	close air support
CCDR	combatant commander
CCJO	Capstone Concept for Joint Operations
CJTF-HOA	Combined Joint Task Force-Horn of Africa
COA	course of action
COG	center of gravity
COIN	counterinsurgency
DLA	Defense Logistics Agency
DMX	decision-making exercise
DO	distributed operations
DOD	Department of Defense
DODD	Department of Defense directive
DOS	Department of State
DOTMLPF	doctrine, organization, training, materiel, leadership and education, personnel, and facilities
HN	host nation
HQ	headquarters
IM	information management
ISR	intelligence, surveillance, and reconnaissance
J-3	operations directorate of a joint staff
J-4	logistics directorate of a joint staff
J-5	plans directorate of a joint staff
J-7	operational plans and interoperability directorate of a joint staff
JALN	joint aerial layer network
JDO	joint distributed operations
JFACC	joint force air component commander
JFC	joint force commander
JFLCC	joint force land component commander
JIATF	joint interagency task force
JIPOE	joint intelligence preparation of the operational environment
JMC	joint movement center
JOA	joint operations area
JOC	joint operating concept
JOE	Joint Operating Environment

JOPP	joint operation planning process
JP	joint publication
JSCC	joint security coordination center
JSO	joint security operations
JSOTF	joint special operations task force
JTF	joint task force
JTF-PO	joint task force-port opening
JWFC	Joint Warfighting Center (USJFCOM)
LNO	liaison officer
LOC	line of communications
LOO	line of operations
MCCDC	Marine Corps Combat Development Command
MCO	Major Combat Operations (a concept name)
MEDEVAC	medical evacuation
NDN	Northern Distribution Network
NRAC	Naval Research Advisory Committee
OPCON	operational control
OPLAN	operation plan
PA	public affairs
PAO	public affairs officer
PCC	policy coordination committee
PD	public diplomacy
PED	processing, exploitation, and dissemination
RFC	revision final coordination
SC	strategic communication
SecDef	Secretary of Defense
SOTF	special operations task force
TACON	tactical control
TTP	tactics, techniques, and procedures
UAV	unmanned aerial vehicle
UAS	unmanned aerial system
US	United States
USCENTCOM	United States Central Command
USF-I	United States Forces-Iraq
USG	United States Government
USJFCOM	United States Joint Forces Command
USTRANSCOM	United States Transportation Command

PART II—TERMS AND DEFINITIONS

area of responsibility. The geographical area associated with a combatant command within which a geographic combatant commander has authority to plan and conduct operations. Also called **AOR**. (JP 3-0)

assessment. A continuous process that measures the overall effectiveness of employing joint force capabilities and the progress toward accomplishing a task, creating an effect, or achieving an objective during military operations. (JP 3-0)

combatant command. A unified or specified command with a broad continuing mission under a single commander established and so designated by the President, through the Secretary of Defense and with the advice and assistance of the Chairman of the Joint Chiefs of Staff. Combatant commands typically have geographic or functional responsibilities. (JP 5-0)

command and control. The exercise of authority and direction by a properly designated commander over assigned and attached forces in the accomplishment of the mission. (JP 3-0)

commander's intent. A clear and concise expression of the operation's purpose and desired end state. (JP 3-0)

communication strategy. A commander's strategy for coordinating and synchronizing themes, messages, images, and actions to support strategic communication objectives and ensure the integrity and consistency of themes and messages to the lowest tactical level. (JP 3-0)

end state. The set of required conditions that defines achievement of the commander's objectives. (JP 3-0)

fires. The use of weapon systems to create a specific lethal or nonlethal effect on a target.

intelligence. The product resulting from the collection, processing, integration, evaluation, analysis, and interpretation of available information concerning foreign nations, hostile or potentially hostile forces or elements, or areas of actual or potential operations. (JP 2-0)

interorganizational partners. A term that includes, but is not limited to, US interagency partners, host nation civilian and military organizations, non-governmental organizations, and international organizations.

joint force. A general term applied to a force composed of significant elements, assigned or attached, of two or more Military Departments operating under a single joint force commander. (JP 3-0)

joint operation planning process. An orderly, analytical process that consists of a logical set of steps to analyze a mission; develop, analyze, and compare alternative courses of action against each other; select the best course of action; and produce a joint operation plan or order. (JP 5-0)

joint task force. A joint force that is constituted and so designated by the Secretary of Defense, a combatant commander, a sub-unified commander, or an existing joint task force commander. Also called **JTF**. (JP 1)

mission command. The conduct of military operations through decentralized execution based upon mission-type orders. (JP 3-0)

maneuver. The employment of forces in the operational area through movement in combination with fires to achieve a position of advantage in respect to the enemy in order to accomplish the mission. (JP 3-0)

operational approach. a visualization of general actions, typically described in text and graphics using lines of effort and lines of operations, to produce conditions that will achieve the desired end state. (JP 5-0)

operational design. The conception and construction of the intellectual framework that underpins joint operation plans and their subsequent execution. (JP 3-0)

operational environment. A composite of the conditions, circumstances, and influences that affect the employment of capabilities and bear on the decisions of the commander. (JP 3-0)

operational limitation. An action required or prohibited by higher authority, such as a constraint or a restraint, and other restrictions that limit the commander's freedom of action, such as diplomatic agreements, rules of engagement, political and economic conditions in affected countries, and host nation issues. (JP 5-0)

protection. The preservation of the effectiveness and survivability of mission-related military and nonmilitary personnel, equipment, facilities, information, and infrastructure deployed or located within or outside the boundaries of a given operational area. (JP 3-0)

strategic communication. Focused United States Government efforts to understand and engage key audiences to create, strengthen, or preserve conditions favorable for the advancement of United States Government interests, policies, and objectives through the use of coordinated programs, plans, themes, messages, and products synchronized with the actions of all instruments of national power. (JP 5-0)

sustainment. The provision of logistics and personnel services required to maintain and prolong operations until successful mission accomplishment. (JP 3-0)

unified action. The synchronization, coordination, and/or integration of the activities of governmental and nongovernmental entities with military operations to achieve unity of effort. (JP 1)

Intentionally Blank

www.ingramcontent.com/pod-product-compliance
Lightning Source LLC
Chambersburg PA
CBHW081329310526
45789CB00018B/2649